YEAR OF
IMPOSSIBLE
GOODBYES

SOOK NYUL CHOI

Houghton Mifflin Company   Boston

To my little brother
and
in memory of my mother and Mark

Library of Congress Cataloging-in-Publication Data

Choi, Sook Nyul.
  Year of impossible goodbyes / Sook Nyul Choi.
    p.   cm.
  Summary: A young Korean girl survives the oppressive Japanese and
Russian occupation of North Korea during the 1940s, to later escape
to freedom in South Korea.
  ISBN 0-395-57419-6
  1. Korea—History—1945- —Juvenile fiction. [1. Korea—
History—1945- —Fiction.]   I. Title.
PZ7.C44626Ye   1991   91-10502
[Fic]—dc20   CIP
                        AC

Printed in the United States of America

QPV 10 9 8 7

Acknowledgments

Throughout the various stages of development of this work, the advice and support of friends and family have been an invaluable source of strength and direction.

I am grateful to Christine Valentine for her encouragement and counsel from the very start. Sven Birkerts and Annabel Betz have my special thanks for their sensitive readings and frank critiques of my early manuscript. The enthusiasm of my friends at the Women's National Book Association was a great encouragement.

I am eternally grateful to my daughters, Kathleen and Audrey, for their endless support and help in bringing this work to fruition. Most of all, I am thankful to my editor, Laura Hornik, for her deep interest in my work.

Sook Nyul Choi
Cambridge, 1991

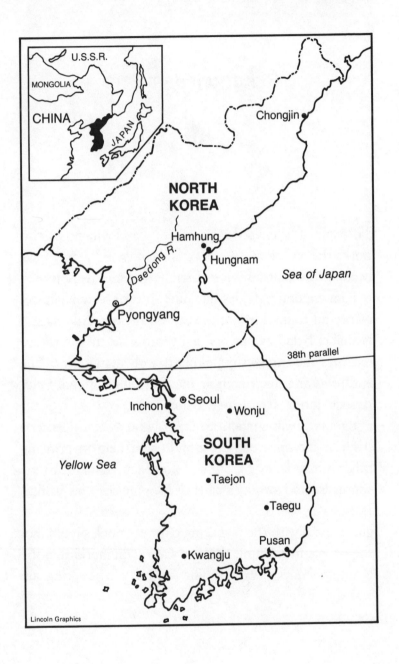

U.S.S.R.

MONGOLIA

CHINA

JAPAN

Chongjin

NORTH
KOREA

Hamhung

Daedong R.

Hungnam

Sea of Japan

Pyongyang

38th parallel

Inchon

Seoul

Wonju

Yellow Sea

SOUTH
KOREA

Taejon

Taegu

Pusan

Kwangju

Lincoln Graphics

Chapter One

Spring 1945

Small clusters of pale green needles emerged from the old weathered pine tree in our front yard. The high mounds of snow in the corner of our yard had begun to melt, the water flowing gently into the furrow of dark earth Grandfather had dug around the base of the tree like a moat. Grandfather's tree stood alone in the far corner of the yard, its dark green-needled branches emanating harmoniously from the trunk, reaching out like a large umbrella. It was a magic tree, holding in the shade of its branches the peace and harmony Grandfather so often talked about.

Despite the warmth of the sun, the air in Kirimni, Pyongyang was dark and heavy, filled with the sound of gunfire and with the menacing glint of drawn swords. For the people in Kirimni, this day was no different from the bitter gray days of winter. The warmth of the spring sun and the thawing of the icy snow brought no respite from the oppressiveness that engulfed us.

Grandfather, hoping the Korean people might experience the exhilaration and beauty of spring again, had made sure my mother included the word *chun,* or spring, in the names of each of my brothers. My oldest brother's name was Hanchun, meaning "Korean spring"; my second brother, Jaechun, was called "spring again"; my third brother, Hyunchun, the "wise spring"; and my youngest brother, Inchun, the "benevolent spring." Inchun was now almost seven, and a benevolent spring still had not come to our village.

I saw Grandfather peer out at the yard from his room, and look at the delicate branches of the pine tree playing against the hazy, pale blue sky. He cleared his throat and called out to Mother. "Hyunsuk, today I will do my morning meditation under the tree."

"But, Father, I've already prepared your place inside," I heard my mother reply in a troubled voice. "Besides," she added, "it isn't warm enough for you yet. Why outside all of a sudden?"

"It is not all of a sudden. Not a single day has gone by that I haven't thought of it. It has been thirty-six years since I have meditated in the warmth of a spring sun. Today, the Japanese soldiers will not keep me inside. I am too old and too tired to be afraid anymore."

Although Mother let out a heavy sigh, she did not protest. Reluctantly, she brought out a clean straw mat and unrolled it beneath the pine tree, placing the thick cushion in the center of the shade. Grandfather emerged from his room and became part of the peaceful scene.

The gentle rays of the April sun flitting through the pine branches played upon his face like dancing fairies.

Excited to see Grandfather meditate beneath his tree, I slid my rice-paper door open a crack and watched. I crossed my legs, resting my hands on my lap with the palms facing up, just as he did. Though his eyes were closed, I kept mine open to watch him. He sat tall and still, like a statue. He looked peaceful as he prayed, yet there was an intensity, an anticipation, in his expression, as though he were waiting for something special to happen. His wrinkles were deep, and I wished that I could run my fingers along the creases in his forehead as he sat motionless in prayer. I wondered what he had to tell the Buddha this morning.

He was still for so long. I began to worry that my Grandfather had been filled with the spirit of the Buddha and had been turned into a statue. I tiptoed outside, quietly crept up toward him, and put my finger under his nose. I felt his faint breath and he coughed gently to reassure me. I sat next to him and watched, happy to be near him. The smell of the pine permeated the atmosphere, and I breathed deeply.

The sun grew stronger as I watched Grandfather, whose shirt of worn gray cloth hung comfortably from his bony shoulders. His crossed legs looked like two bent chopsticks. His handsome face was sad, peaceful, intent, but always dignified.

The women in town called him "Patriot Grandfather" or "Scholar Grandfather." Sometimes they brought special letters or poetry written in Chinese characters for Grandfather to translate into Korean script, *Hangul.* During my first lesson with Grandfather, he had shown me how to write his name. With his oxtail brush, he swiftly drew two large Chinese characters on a large piece of soft white rice paper. *"Yong-Wun,"* he explained, meant "Dragon Cloud." With a few fluid strokes, his brush created an island of billowy clouds hovering over the mountains. When I looked at the picture more carefully, I saw there was a gentle dragon resting on a cloud, peering down upon the earth. Grandfather told me the dragon is a symbol of good fortune and dignity. Presiding over rain and water, the dragon works to save the crops during times of drought and bring abundance and prosperity to the people.

Grandfather opened his eyes and looked at me as if he knew I had been staring at him. I was disappointed to see him stir; time would no longer stand still. He looked deep into my eyes, and then smiled, happy that we had celebrated this spring day together in such a special way. We got up and hurried inside to start our morning lessons.

While I had my lesson, Mother and Inchun stayed in the yard to prepare for the girls who would be arriving to work at the sock factory. If the Japanese police came by, Mother or Inchun would rap on the door, signaling for us to put away our books. As a Korean child, I wasn't supposed to be learning any of the Korean or Chinese that Grandfather was teaching me. I was almost ten and should have been in Japanese school. But as I was small

4

for my age, Mother had been able to avoid registering me for the first grade when the police came by last spring. Mother kept hoping that the war would end, and that at least Inchun and I would be spared from attending Japanese school. All my older brothers and my sister had had to go.

I was glad to be home with Grandfather, reading and writing Korean and learning about the ancient Korean kingdoms. My favorite parts of the lesson were reading ancient Chinese poetry and practicing brush writing. But our forty-minute lesson went by too quickly. The police would soon be coming by to remind us to make our morning offerings at the Shinto temple. We were to pray for the good health of the Heavenly Emperor and for success in the war against the "White Devils." This marked the beginning of each dreary day under the watchful eyes of the Imperial police.

Grandfather closed his thick, weathered Chinese text, and I went out to the yard to help Mother. I looked at our small house with its curved roof of gray clay tile and thought what a beautiful house it could be if we had the time to decorate it and plant a flower garden. Instead, a big, ugly wooden shack dominated the yard. It had been there for as long as I could remember. Built under the orders of the Japanese, it served as a factory to manufacture socks for the Japanese soldiers and merchants. My mother was in charge of the factory and supervised the young women who worked from early morning until late evening on the old knitting machines.

To shut out the sight of that ugly shack, I rested my eyes on the tree that stood in the far corner. A low stone wall ran behind the tree; the wooden gate stood slightly ajar. I wished that wall and gate could keep the Japanese police away from us. It was our gate and our house, yet the Japanese tromped in and out whenever they wanted to without so much as a knock.

Later that morning, Captain Narita came walking through the gate. He paced about the yard, his sword hanging from his small wiry frame. His thick gold-rimmed glasses magnified his cold probing glance. The sun reflected off the handle of his sword, the rims of his glasses, and his gold and red epaulets. A smile played upon his lips as he examined us with apparent disdain. Mother had always told me to go quietly inside whenever Captain Narita and his men came to the house, but this time I just stood and looked at him.

"You did not go to Shinto temple yet," he said to Mother.

She looked him in the eye and responded in perfect Japanese. "We will go very soon. But for now we have to prepare tea and millet crackers for the girls so that they can make many socks for the Imperial soldiers. The girls come from far away, and on empty stomachs they will not be able to make so many socks."

Captain Narita eyed Mother from head to toe. It was considered a serious offense even to look at the Imperial police; Koreans were expected to keep their heads bowed and obey orders unconditionally. The girls at the sock

6

factory told me that Mother was probably the only person who could talk to Captain Narita and get away with it.

Stroking his mustache with one hand and his sword with the other, he said, "Then you make sure that all the girls make their offerings to our Heavenly Emperor and pray for the defeat of the White Devils." Flanked by his two ever-present lieutenants, he strode toward the sock factory. Their swords and guns clanked against their belts in an all-too-familiar rhythm as they strutted past me. They inspected the inside of the factory and spoke briefly to my cousin Kisa, the mechanic, who arrived early each morning to grease the machines. They then walked straight through the yard and out the front gate, without inspecting the house.

We were all relieved to see them leave, and Mother set the table with a pot of cool barley tea and a tray of small millet cookies. "One day I would just love to surprise these poor hard-working girls with some delicious white rice cakes instead of coarse yellow millet cakes," said Aunt Tiger, who lived with us.

Mother sighed. "Our farmers make enough rice to feed all of us, yet we must eat millet and barley. All that rice goes to feed the Imperial soldiers and the Japanese residents . . . some even gets sent back to Japan . . . and the prices they charge us for the little rice that remains! Did you see the look of satisfaction on Captain Narita's face as he looked at these coarse little cookies?"

Just then, Haiwon came rushing through the gate. Although she lived far away, she was always the first of

7

the girls to arrive. She wanted to have as much time as possible with us, and so always tried to arrive here early. As usual, she carried her bag from which the wooden knitting needles Grandfather had whittled for her poked out. As soon as she sat, she started to eat and drink her portion of tea and millet cookies while knitting and talking all at the same time.

Haiwon loved the millet cakes and ate them as if they were the most delicious delicacies. Unlike her plain gray outfit, she had a vibrant, energetic personality. She was so full of life that she made us all forget everything. We watched and listened in amazement. It seemed as if in the ten hours that she was away from us, she did nothing but gather information and stories to tell us. Each day, she had something new to make us laugh.

My mother sat opposite her and asked about her mother's health. Haiwon fell silent, then murmured, "My mother will never get better until she sees my brothers. She is losing her mind. She now even bows to the Shinto god and asks him to send her boys back to her." Looking around at my mother, she then whispered timidly, "Are the Japanese really a divine race, as they all teach us? Is their emperor really a god?"

Mother sighed and said firmly, "Of course not. They are all human beings just like us, all children of one God."

"You mean your Catholic God that you pray to every night?" Aunt Tiger interrupted. "Well, your God is silent and sleeping while the Japanese are busy torturing and killing us Koreans. We are as helpless as flies and it is getting worse as the war goes on."

Mother saw me listening intently, and shot a disapproving glance at Aunt Tiger. "The war will be over soon," Mother said firmly. "I hear the Japanese are not doing well. All will be fine, you'll see."

Then Okja arrived and silently took her place at the table. Okja, almost twenty, was very tall, and next to Haiwon, she looked like a telephone pole. Unlike Haiwon, she ate nothing and spoke very little. Soon the rest of the girls rushed in, grabbed the cookies and tea, and chattered like magpies.

At precisely eight o'clock, the loud clanging filled the air. How sad I was when Kisa rang that fateful bell. The girls instantly fell silent and ran to their assigned seats in the factory. Lined up on two long benches, the girls sat as though glued to their machines like puppets for the rest of the day. The yard was suddenly quiet and empty. There was nobody for me to talk to. Inchun preferred to play with his top, making it spin and jump, or to draw beautiful pictures, using the dirt yard as his canvas and a broken twig as his paintbrush. He played quietly and would only occasionally nod or shrug his shoulders in response to me. But every once in a while, he would smile broadly, flashing his dimples.

I often envied my little brother, for he spent a good part of the day with Grandfather, whittling, tying knots of all shapes, and making netted bags for Mother to carry things in. Because I was four years older, I had to help

Mother and Aunt Tiger in the sock factory. Because I was a girl, I was supposed to stay with the women. I wasn't supposed to disturb Grandfather after my morning lesson. How I wished I could be with them.

I looked at the quiet, deserted yard and began cleaning up the breakfast table. Then, I helped Mother and Aunt Tiger inspect the socks, fold them, and pack them. I asked how long Mother had been running the sock factory. "If it wasn't socks, it was something else," she said. "For over thirty years I've been working for the Japanese. Lately they don't even pay us the little money they used to. For the last three weeks we have all worked without any pay. If they don't pay us soon with money or rice, we will all go hungry."

"They're very clever," Aunt Tiger said bitterly. "They keep us so hungry that we can't do anything but worry about where our next meal is coming from. They keep us hungry for so long that we are grateful for whatever little food we get."

I got up and went to the factory. I wanted to see Kisa and the girls even though I knew they would have no time for me. I didn't want to hear what Mother and Aunt Tiger talked about, and I was sorry I had asked any questions.

The rhythm of the machines whirring and clanking in the sock factory made me forget everything. I gazed at the two rows of girls. Their heads were bent and their shoulders hunched as they reached out to grab the threads with one hand and hold the wheel of the machines with the other. The spools of thread spun frenetically as the needles of the machines bobbed up and down. These girls were entangled in machines that would never set them free.

I remembered how fascinated I was when I was first allowed to come and watch the girls amidst the whirring machines and the long knit tubes. It amazed me to see the skeins of thread hanging in midair, suspended by wires strung across the ceiling. The girls constantly pedaled in a desperate attempt to complete their work, as the snake-like knit tubes emerged from the machines and fell at their ankles. I pretended the spools of threads were flying puppets in the sky, the girls magicians, and Kisa, standing on the platform high above them, the master of this grand act.

Kisa, the only male in the factory, watched the spools and machines from his viewing stand to make sure all ran smoothly. The girls raced against time to meet their quotas. If the lights went out or the leather belts fell out of the grooves of the wheels, the girls panicked, for that meant they would have to stay until all hours to complete their work.

I sat in the factory and looked forward to the evening, when I might be able to talk to my favorite sock girls. By that time, their eyes would be half closed and their whole bodies covered with a layer of gray cotton residue, their lips parched from cutting small threads with their teeth to save time. There was no time to look for the one pair of scissors that all fifteen of them had to share.

I walked around the factory and peered at the girls. I could see only their profiles as they bent over their work. No one looked up. Some I knew very well and some I barely knew at all. Because there was so little time, it was hard to get to know them, unless they were very talkative. Most girls did not stay with us for very long anyway; Captain Narita made sure of that. But for some reason Haiwon and Okja must have escaped his notice, for they had been with us for quite a while.

Kisa waved from his viewing stand and motioned that I could come up to see him. He rarely allowed me up there with him, so I was in heaven. Everything looked different from where he stood. The spools of thread looked like hats atop the girls' heads. But after a few minutes, Kisa smiled. I knew it was time to get down before Mother saw me. She thought it was too dangerous for me to be up on a small platform with no railing. Kisa whispered, "There is always tomorrow. You can talk to the girls tomorrow, and serve them tea." I went down somewhat consoled as I thought of what we might talk about.

How nice Kisa was. I always felt a little sorry for him. Something was wrong with one of his legs, causing him to limp awkwardly. He had also lost a couple of fingers on his right hand while working at a machine. But he had a very pleasant broad forehead, which Mother said was a sign of a generous heart, and he had a handsome nose, a sign of an even temperament, Mother said. His friendly twinkling eyes were unusual for a Korean man. The light in his eyes danced as he looked at you and you just had to smile back as you listened to his deep gentle voice. We all loved him, and were happy he had not been taken away to a labor camp, as my three brothers and most of the other men in our town had been. As Father's nephew, he tried very hard to fill my father's place. Although Mother told him he was doing the job of four men by being here to help all of us women, Kisa wished that he could be working with my father in Manchuria in the Korean independence movement.

I went back out to the yard to help Mother and Aunt Tiger. We spread out the long tubes that the girls had made, cut them, and sewed them on one end, turning them into tube socks. While I worked, I looked at my mother's fair oval face and her large almond-shaped eyes which glowed softly behind the fatigue and sorrow. I followed the tiny wrinkles around her eyes and neck. But her hands, which moved so quickly as she repaired the stitches the machines had missed, distracted me. Her long thin fingers were dry and chapped, and full of callused needle marks. I once heard from the girls in the factory that Mother was known as the beauty of her hometown, and I tried to picture how pretty Mother must have been.

In silence, I continued to work, now fixing my gaze on the shadows the tree cast around us. Although I loved this pine tree, I longed for some flowers like we used to have when I was very small. We were not allowed to spend time cultivating the garden anymore. Captain Narita said flowers did not help the soldiers at the front; we must spend every waking moment trying to help them in the battle against the White Devils. Once, when we did manage to have a tiny patch of flowers, Captain Narita's police stepped through them as they grinned broadly. There was nothing we could do but watch as the dainty flowers were crushed beneath their ugly boots.

After that, Mother put her packets of seeds away, carefully wrapped in rice paper. Sometimes I opened the packages to look at the seeds. Each time I opened the carefully wrapped packets, the paper in which they were wrapped seemed more yellow and brittle. I wondered if we would ever be able to plant those seeds.

I can still remember years ago when Mother picked the wilted clusters of bright crimson azalea petals from our little garden. In a bowl, she gently ground the petals with a pestle until they turned into a fragrant red paste. Then she made ten tiny balls of paste and put one on each of my fingernails. I sat very still with my fingers spread as far apart as I could to make it easier for Mother. She wrapped each fingernail with a large sesame leaf and tied each fingertip carefully with red yarn, trying not to let the red paste touch any of the skin of my fingers. I went around all day with my fingers spread apart so as not to disturb anything. I looked as if I was carrying ten precious little packages, one on the tip of each finger, and Mother smiled. That night I went to sleep with my arms stretched out to the sides so that none of the sesame leaves would come off. The scent of faint azaleas and sesame leaves filled the room, and I went to sleep swearing not to move an inch.

Of course, some of the sesame wrappers had come off by morning and some of the pink liquid had run down my fingers. Mother and I laughed. Not only my nails, but a few of my fingers were entirely red. But after washing them very carefully for several days, only my fingernails remained a deep pretty pink. I showed my elegantly decorated fingernails to everyone. Later, I watched with fascination as my nails grew out.

I had once told Aunt Tiger about my pretty pink nails, hoping that she and I could venture out and plant a secret garden somewhere. She just looked at me and repeated what Captain Narita had said. "Korean women have no time for that nonsense." Then she sighed and said, "When the war is over you can plant the whole yard with flowers." She went to her room and brought me a bundle wrapped in a yellowed handkerchief. I opened it and saw packages of seeds with pictures of sunflowers, pansies, and many other flowers that I could not identify. I kept them together with Mother's packets to plant when the Japanese left. I knew Mother would find some azaleas somehow.

Mother looked at me and smiled. She didn't know what I was daydreaming about. Or maybe she did. "Doesn't this pine tree smell good?" she said. "It's like a different world sitting beneath this tree." I smiled and nodded. We didn't talk of the flowers and garden we could not have.

I looked at Aunt Tiger, who was unusually quiet. She was very different from Mother, who was tall, slender, and elegant. Aunt Tiger was stocky and round. She didn't go quietly about her duties, always trying to make the best of everything, as Mother did. She spoke her mind, and often complained bitterly. I thought it refreshing to hear her complain, for she so often said what I was feeling.

At night Aunt usually grew sad and pensive. She didn't get angry or complain about our lives or about the cruelty of the Japanese. Instead, she told the most wonderful stories about the animals that lived in the forests of Korea long ago. All the wild animals in her fables talked as if they were human. She was especially fond of telling stories of the majestic tigers that used to roam the Korean mountains until the Japanese hunted them down for their skins.

Aunt told us so many wonderful stories of these clever talking tigers that we began calling her Aunt Tiger. I could never forget the tears in her eyes as she told us about the mother tiger who roamed the mountains in search of her cubs, not knowing they had been killed by hunters. Her voice trembled as she spoke, and I felt as if she were talking about her own babies. As I looked into her mournful eyes, I wondered if she complained so bitterly to hide her sorrow from us. She didn't want to be weak, and I knew how strong she was. It was a different kind of strength from Mother's.

As we worked, the sun began to set and darkness fell. The whirring of the machines suddenly stopped and I heard the low murmuring of the girls as they emerged from the factory and stretched their stiff, aching muscles. Mother, Kisa, and Aunt wished them a safe trip home. The tired girls looked sad but relieved to have made it through another day. They bowed to Mother in silence, and Mother watched with concern as their weary gray figures disappeared into the liberation of darkness.

Mother, Aunt, and Kisa then went into the factory to put the socks in neat piles for the Japanese merchants and police. Inchun and I busied ourselves putting heavy blankets over the rice-paper paneled doors of our room. We lit a candle and in the small pool of dancing light, we looked at Grandfather's Chinese books and Mother's book of American fairy tales. Then I started to read aloud from one of our books written in Korean script, *Hangul*. Mother joined us later with a pile of socks that needed mending before the morning, and listened to me read to Inchun. She carefully checked all the work done that day, for she didn't want any of the girls to be in trouble with the police.

Soon, Inchun got tired of listening to me read and started dozing. His books fell from his little hands, his mouth fell open, and he began to snore softly.

I kept reading and tried hard to stay awake until Mother was finished with her work. I watched her at night as intently as I watched my Grandfather in the morning. She took off her gray outfit and put on her long white gown. Then she reached back to pull out the tarnished pin that held her braided hair in a large twisted knot at the nape of her neck. When Mother pulled out the little silver pin, her long braided hair came tumbling down like a big heavy rope. It almost touched the floor as she sat on her knees. When she finished unbraiding her hair, she slowly combed the wavy mass. In her white night gown, with her long wavy hair framing her face, she looked like an entirely different person. It was easy to see how Mother had once been the town beauty as the sock girls had said.

While she quietly combed the mass of wavy hair, I played with her tarnished silver pin. Though it looked like a cheap piece of metal, it was actually a beautifully crafted silver hairpin. When I looked closely, I could see a multitude of embossed little roses and small birds flying. I touched the pin with my finger tips and felt the grooves of the tiny rose petals and the little bumps of the birds' wings. I held it in my palm, and reveled in its cool smoothness. I tossed it into the air and caught it again.

"Mother," I asked, "why not shine it so that all these birds and rose petals can sparkle in the sunlight? It's so pretty."

Mother sighed and said, "It is beautiful, isn't it? It was done by a silversmith for my mother when I was little. Both the silversmith and my mother died in a fire set by the Japanese soldiers. But somehow I managed to find it on the ground when I returned to the site of my old home. It was buried in the mud, but it caught my eye for it shone so brilliantly in the sun. I want to keep it as long as I can, and if it were polished, Captain Narita and his lieutenants might notice it and take it away. We would be in trouble for not having offered it long ago for the melting pot."

As I stared sadly at the pin in my palm, Mother brushed my hair from my forehead. "When the war is over and the Japanese leave, you can polish it and you can fix my hair with it. For now hide the books away and blow the candle out. We must sleep and save the candle for tomorrow night."

Chapter Two

One hot, muggy day in June, while Inchun and I sat working on the tube socks, Aunt Tiger and Mother told us they had a plan. We were going to have a special surprise celebration for Haiwon's sixteenth birthday. Aunt Tiger insisted she would make a visit to my sister Theresa's convent to get one of those fancy books the nuns decorated with pictures of saints and angels. That would surely be something very special for Haiwon. Mother hesitated. It was her daughter, after all. "I'll go myself," she said. "You don't know the back route as I do."

The convent was in the countryside just outside of Pyongyang City. It was only twenty minutes away by train, but the Japanese Imperial police forbade anyone from traveling, so Mother had to go by foot on back roads. She really didn't want to go empty-handed; she had nothing to bring them. "But perhaps it is about time," Mother decided. "Maybe they will have some news about the war." The nuns often knew much more than the rest of us because of the radio hidden in the basement of the convent, and the occasional contact they had with American priests.

The next day, Mother left right after the police made their morning inspection in order to be able to return before dark. We all hoped that the Imperial police would not come back later in the day and notice her absence. Mother did so much work at the sock factory that the days when she went to the convent were extra busy for all of us. Kisa, Aunt Tiger, and I ran around twice as fast to get the work done. Even little Inchun and Grandfather came out to the yard to make it look busier in case the police suddenly appeared.

I wished I could have gone with Mother to see Theresa and the other nuns. Theresa, my oldest sibling, had entered the convent when I was very little. I remember visiting her there. She looked like a penguin in her long black gown and the little white veil on her head. But that was long ago. For the past two years, Mother had gone to see her alone. She said that most of the day was spent coming and going and the visit with Theresa and the nuns was very brief. It would be too much walking for me, and it was dangerous. If we were caught by the police, we would be questioned and punished for disobeying orders, and above all, for going to worship any other god than the Shinto god.

We all worried about Mother's safety when she left on these trips, but we knew how much she loved going to see the nuns. "Your mother would risk almost anything to see her firstborn at the convent," said Aunt Tiger. Mother always told us Theresa was an important part of all of our lives even though she was far away from us. I often wished that she were here so that I could talk to her. I remembered when Theresa told me how much she loved all of us. But if she loved us that much, why did she live so far away in that big house with strangers all dressed like penguins?

"That is the way it's supposed to be," said Mother. "God wanted Theresa to be a nun and she answered His call." I wondered if God would ever call me as He had called Theresa.

We were sorting the socks and tying them into bundles when Mother returned late that evening. "The Reverend Mother said the Japanese were doing poorly in the war," Mother said, picking up a pile of socks to examine. "The nuns are praying night and day for their defeat." Aunt Tiger looked at me, rolled her eyes, and left the room. She didn't think much of the nuns' prayers. But Aunt Tiger was glad to see that Mother had brought a small bag of pure white rice, just enough to make a few rice cookies. Mother didn't bring back any records this time, but she did have a small book of Christian stories full of pictures of colorful winged angels in Heaven. "You can look at it," Mother said to Inchun and me, "then you can wrap it up for Haiwon."

Inchun grabbed the book from me and ran into his room. I followed him and together we read the book. He got some paper and copied the pictures of the angels. I copied the passages and we made our own copy of this little book. We had to wrap it for Haiwon, but we wanted to make it special, so we took out a piece of white rice paper that Grandfather had given us, and drew lots of pictures and made our own fancy wrapping paper.

It was late at night and our rice-paper paneled doors were draped with thick blankets. We were all busy planning for Haiwon's birthday celebration. We heard Grandfather moving about in his room, and Mother and Aunt Tiger busy in the kitchen. Soon Kisa came by to check on us, and told us to turn off the lights. I felt too excited to go to sleep. Haiwon would be *so* surprised. I lay in the dark wishing it were morning.

The next morning I couldn't wait until Haiwon opened our little present wrapped with the special paper. The table was set much earlier than usual. Grandfather didn't meditate this morning. Even little Inchun was out early in the yard helping us. Instead of the few millet cookies and kettle of barley tea that usually awaited the girls, there was now a banquet for Haiwon. It was really a very humble feast, but a special occasion for us, since we had never before dared to have such a celebration. The little brass bowls with their matching tops had been brightly polished, and were now filled with hot soup. The brass plates held a few tiny white rice cookies, and the brass chopsticks shone in the sunlight. I could smell the hot beef broth, which we hadn't been able to have for a long time. We looked forward to the few minutes we could celebrate with Haiwon before the other girls arrived. Above all, we had to put everything away before the Imperial police came.

Haiwon came racing in looking as if she had just tumbled out of bed. She must have really rushed to arrive so early. She wore a worried expression as if she were thinking, "Is there something wrong? Didn't the soldiers like the socks I made?" Smiling, Mother met her and escorted her to her seat where the pretty package awaited her. She looked stunned when Mother told her that all this was in her honor, and she sat motionless. "Hurry and open your presents," Mother said. "We don't have much time."

As Haiwon opened her gift, her fingers trembled and tears began to well up in her eyes. She held the little book ever so tightly against her breast and she straightened the wrapping paper to see the drawings. She carefully rolled up the paper and put it in her bag. Inchun and I were happy to know that she liked our humble present as much as the little book. She bowed to Mother as she tried to hold back her tears. Haiwon's embarrassed delight made her look beautiful. Her face was flushed and for once she was speechless and remained silent long enough for me to see how pretty the shape of her mouth was. She seemed full of happy thoughts. Looking around me, I felt a big lump in my throat. As Haiwon wiped away her tears, she got up again and made another deep bow to Mother.

Then I saw Grandfather slowly come out of his room smiling. Haiwon was special to him. He and Haiwon's father had been good friends. Long ago, Mother had said to me, "I wish I could keep her and her mother with us. Your grandfather and Haiwon's father go back a long way.

Your grandfather used to teach Haiwon's father and his sons." Haiwon became even more flustered upon seeing Grandfather. She knew the honor that was being bestowed upon her. She got up and bowed deeply. Grandfather motioned for her to sit down and gave her a small package. Mother nudged her and said, "Quickly now . . . we are running out of time." Haiwon unrolled the scroll of white rice paper. Grandfather had painted a beautiful winged horse flying toward the sky. Underneath it there were two Chinese characters in his fine calligraphy that said "thousand patience" and her name in *Hangul*. At Mother's urging, we ate hurriedly while the morning sun rose.

We lifted the lids of our soup bowls. The brass dishes were lovely and we each had a sliver of meat in our soup. Haiwon ate quickly in silence, trying to savor every taste. She hesitated to take a bite of the rice cake for a second and Mother said, "That is yours . . . eat it now. I saved one for you to take home for your mother." We were very happy to see Haiwon enjoy this small treat as if it were the biggest banquet she had ever seen. Haiwon's smile made us all feel this was a grand day. I wished Kisa were here, but he was busy cleaning and greasing Haiwon's machine especially for her. We were all so happy that for a few moments, we forgot the Imperial police. We laughed and ate. It was enchanting for me. I felt I was in a faraway land where there were no worries of any kind. The warm June breeze touched my cheek and I couldn't remember ever having had such a good time.

Suddenly, I saw the gate to our yard swing open. I froze. Captain Narita and his two lieutenants quietly came marching into our yard. It was still much too early for them to be coming by, but there they were. At that moment, I could not help feeling that maybe they *were* gods. How could they possibly know when to appear? How did they know this was a special time for us? How?

Mother looked pale. Her eyes were fixed on Grandfather. Haiwon started to cry hysterically. The captain walked to our humble wooden table, and his sword clanked against his belt as he approached. The two lieutenants stood behind us and looked at our table in disbelief.

For a moment or two they were silent. Captain Narita eyed all the brassware and with his sword swept everything to the ground. The brass dishes, chopsticks, and soup spoons clanked against each other as they went tumbling. He saw the knitting bag resting against Haiwon's chair, and he motioned to one of his lieutenants. Haiwon's presents were opened and shown to the Captain. He looked at Grandfather's beautiful brush painting and at the little book. Captain Narita quietly signaled for these to be taken away. "Where did you get this?" he coolly inquired. Nobody answered. Haiwon sobbed uncontrollably. Captain Narita then looked at Grandfather, who sat with his eyes closed like a stone statue.

Stroking his mustache, Captain Narita paced around the table where we remained seated. The best thing to do when he came was to lower one's eyes and wait. I had heard that many times from the sock girls, but I had to look at him. Except for Grandfather's and mine, everyone's eyes were lowered in silence.

Captain Narita whispered in a chilling monotone, "So, you are doing something on your own again. Did you forget that there is a war going on and that we must do all we can to help the Imperial soldiers fight the White Devils?" Then he looked at Mother and said, "Metal is not for your use. The soldiers need it for weapons. The dishes must be sent to my office at once."

Then he walked over to my grandfather and glared at him. Grandfather remained seated erect with his eyes closed and his jaw set. Captain Narita stared at my grandfather for a long time and, looking at Mother's pale face, he said, "When will you stupid Koreans understand that you are our subjects and there is nothing we, the Imperial police of the Heavenly race, do not know about your activities. There is nothing we cannot do. If you value this old man's life, you'd better remember that you are our subjects."

He smiled with satisfaction and walked out as calmly as he had come in. One of his lieutenants had Haiwon's presents tucked under his arm. The other told us they would be back for the metal dishes and we had better have them cleaned and prepared for pickup. For them it was as if nothing out of the ordinary had occurred.

No one said a word. Grandfather opened his eyes and pensively stared down at his hands for a while. Then I noticed he was trembling. His face was pale, gloomy. He looked angry and humiliated. I had never seen him like this. I didn't know what to do. Mother and Aunt Tiger rushed to help him indoors, but he pushed both of them away. "I can go in alone," he said. "I shall never come out again. Throw my shoes away."

I hated Captain Narita for doing this to my aged grandfather. Was there no respect for one's elders?

Haiwon continued to sob hysterically, blaming herself and apologizing to Mother. "No, no," said Mother. "It isn't anyone's fault. Captain Narita has been doing this all his life in Korea. Every time he squeezes a little tighter." Mother hugged Haiwon and comforted her and promised her a real birthday party after the war was over. Then she went to see Grandfather.

Meanwhile, Aunt Tiger started picking up the bowls. "I didn't like the way Captain Narita left so quietly. He has something up his sleeve," she said.

Aunt Tiger was right. That afternoon two young Japanese-trained Korean police came into our yard and told Mother that they had come to chop down the pine tree. Aunt Tiger muttered with disgust, *"Chin-il-pa,"* which means friend of Japan, or traitor. The two young boys stared down at the ground in silence.

"Let them be," said Mother to Aunt Tiger. "They have to do whatever they're told. Let the Japanese have the tree. They can cut it down or dig it up or do whatever they want. What does it matter." Aunt Tiger looked even angrier. She started to wail and pound on her chest with her fists. Mother grabbed Aunt Tiger, pulled her inside, and said harshly, "Stop that! Stop it! Don't let the Japanese have your soul. We can't let them make us crazy. That is exactly what they want."

Aunt Tiger continued to cry bitterly as the police began hacking our tree to pieces. I wondered how Captain Narita knew that destroying the tree was the best way to punish Grandfather for writing Chinese and *Hangul.*

When the tree had been hacked to pieces, the young policemen left. Mother and Aunt Tiger were inside taking care of Grandfather. Mother sent Kisa to fetch a Buddhist monk. If we were lucky, the monk would visit us at night with his herbal medicine. I was told to stay in my room, but I sat outside Grandfather's door. It was quiet in his room, but I heard Aunt Tiger sobbing softly and whispering to Mother, "The Imperial police love making Koreans hurt each other. They let the Koreans do all the dirty work and then tell us 'You Koreans do it to yourselves; we Imperial soldiers do no such thing.'" Mother said nothing.

I didn't want to listen anymore, and I went out and looked at the scattered branches of our beautiful pine tree. I stared at the sharp pine needles. I wished that all these pine needles would turn into real needles and prick the horrible Imperial soldiers. Then I felt guilty. Mother would not be pleased with me for having such wicked thoughts. I picked up some of the branches and held them close to my heart, hoping they would magically comfort me. I wanted to do something with these branches. I couldn't bring them into Grandfather's room. Every morning Mother cut a few branches and arranged them in his room. But now it was different. Tears of anger, confusion, and frustration rolled down my cheeks. I cried until I could hardly breathe, tasting my own salty tears as they streamed down my face.

For the first time, I did not like being a Korean child. I knew from Grandfather's history lessons that in the olden days of the Paekche and the Silla kingdoms, many Korean scholars, artists, and Buddhist priests had gone to Japan to teach the Japanese about Buddhism, architecture, and Korean arts and culture. The Korean nobility had been welcomed guests among the Japanese, who were eager to use Korea as a bridge to Chinese culture. Grandfather had told me many times we were a people of nobility and culture, and I should always be very proud to be Korean. But suddenly, I was sorry that I was born a Korean child. I wished that I were Japanese. I thought of the Japanese children who went to the special school and lived in pretty houses that Koreans used to own. The Japanese could have whatever they wanted in Korea.

But then, I noticed that Inchun had come out to the yard and was sitting by me. He looked so bewildered, I was suddenly ashamed. He looked tired, scared, and lost. I was his *nuna*, his big sister, and I had to do something. I hurriedly wiped away my tears. As I mustered an awkward smile, I quickly said, "You know what? These branches smell so good. Let's give them to the sock girls. I know they don't even have time to talk to us, but they can smell the pine as they work. Those mean soldiers did us a favor after all. We always said we wanted to give the sock girls something. These branches are small and are the perfect size for them to take home. The tree will grow again. Let's water the roots first." I was happy to see my little brother's eyes sparkle through his tears. I saw him run inside to the kitchen to grab a wooden bucket for fetching water. Looking at that wooden bucket, I thought of how we would have to go back to using wooden chopsticks and dishes tomorrow. I decided not to think of the future.

When Inchun returned, we watered the tree stump, filled the wooden bucket with branches of pine, and went over to the sock factory. How noisy and dusty it was. Inchun and I put some pine branches next to each girl's bag. They quickly smiled without looking up. When I came to Haiwon, I left a big branch.

Inchun and I sat outside on the stump of the pine tree. It made a nice chair for the two of us. We sat back to back, so we wouldn't fall off. Pushing against each other, each of us tried to make the other fall off and we laughed. I looked up at the sky. I thought of how nicely and evenly the tree used to branch out, and how I had sat with Grandfather and watched the shadows of the pine needles dance about him. I was glad that he had not witnessed his beloved tree being so brutally destroyed. I looked up at the sky and tried not to cry, but I couldn't keep from thinking of what he had said about no longer needing his shoes.

Chapter Three

Grandfather didn't come out to the yard to meditate the next morning. I hoped he would forget about what he had said, and I stood staring at the gray stone stoop where he had left his white rubber shoes. I longed to see his calm meditative expression. But when I looked at the ugly stump that remained, I was relieved that Grandfather was not there to see what had become of his beloved pine tree. I was sure he had heard them chop it down, but I was glad that he didn't have to see it.

Everything had changed overnight! Captain Narita and his men had such power over our lives. I couldn't help but wonder if the Japanese truly were a divine race. Had we Koreans done something to deserve this cruelty? I saw Mother running out of the kitchen toward the sock factory. As she passed Grandfather's shoes, she placed them facing out toward the yard so that they would be ready for him.

I wanted to ask Mother about the Japanese. But I knew she wouldn't answer me. She would say what she always said: "You are a little girl, and there is nothing for you to worry about. Just do as you are told. Soon all will be well. God is watching over us." I thought of asking Aunt Tiger, but I had tried asking her before. "It's bad enough that we have to live under them," she said. "Who wants to talk about it? There's no time for inquisitive children now. Don't bother your Grandfather with these questions either. He was tortured for so long by the Japanese — you shouldn't make him talk about it; it will only cause him pain to think of such things." Since that time I never did ask Grandfather about the Japanese. Besides, once a lesson began, I was happy learning what Grandfather taught me. There was so much to learn and so little time. But now I wished that I had asked him. I wished I hadn't listened to Aunt Tiger.

While I was brooding in my room and blaming Aunt for my frustrations, she dashed into my room and startled me. "Grandfather feels a little better now and has asked for you," she said with urgency. "Hurry . . . just listen to him, and don't ask him anything." I had to contain my anger as we rushed to Grandfather's room. Mother brought Inchun, who sat next to me and whispered, "Mother said to tell you we're not supposed to ask any questions . . . just listen." I nodded sadly, seeing how pale and thin Grandfather looked. Aunt Tiger, tired and somber, left the room. Mother remained quietly in the corner. I could tell they had been up all night watching Grandfather.

Inchun and I waited in silence for him to speak. He lay quietly as though asleep. After a long while, he opened his eyes a little and smiled faintly. "Come closer, sit by me," he said, his eyes closing again. Inchun and I put our hands into the cool bony hand he stretched toward us. He squeezed our hands tightly for just a few seconds. There was a peacefulness that graced the room and I felt calm being with him.

Mother stood in the doorway, watching his every movement. She came to his bedside and placed his arm back under the blanket. She wanted him to rest. But then, as if ordered to do so, she said, "Your grandfather insists on talking to you both, especially you, Sookan." She looked into my eyes with great concern. I could tell she wanted me just to listen and not to prolong the visit. I nodded to assure her. She stepped back and stood in the corner. I looked at my grandfather. His silver hair that had flown wildly in the wind and glistened in the morning sun was now combed neatly back. Every strand of hair stood in place with lifeless perfection. How I wished I could ruffle it up and blow on it to see it dance.

Inchun and I sat on the *ondol,* the coal-heated floor covered with glazed rice paper. We sat there by his thick blanket for a long time and waited for him to speak. I listened to the sound of his gentle breath. Time seemed to stand still. The room had a faint scent of pine from the branches that Mother had arranged daily in the little bowl on his desk. I looked over at his scholar's desk with its many mysterious drawers. It was draped with some drab gray cloth to conceal it from the Imperial police, but I knew by heart its beautiful carvings depicting Buddhist

monks and temples. Hidden in the drawers were Grandfather's oxtail brushes, the ink slate, and the books of
Chinese poetry.

Though his eyes were still closed, I could tell by the
way the little muscles under his eyelids twitched ever so
gently that he was thinking. Then, slowly opening his
eyes, he said softly, "How good you children are. Your
Mother taught you well. You are patient, respectful, and
wise beyond your years." It was the first time Grandfather
had ever complimented us. Usually he taught us how and
what to do. If he was pleased, he would simply smile, or
would occasionally pat us on the head. I was overwhelmed by such praise and my face burned with embar-
rassment. Instead of vehemently denying this praise as I
should have done, I said nothing as I promised Mother
not to talk. I looked at her, and saw that she too was
flushed, touched to hear such unexpected compliments
from her own father.

Grandfather whispered, "Do not feel bitter about what
happened. I am not angry anymore. I know that better
times will soon come to you." His voice was growing
weaker. He looked at all of us and motioned for Inchun
and me to draw closer. His voice barely audible, he said,
"You should know some stories about your family. Not just
the ancient history I taught you, and not just those Bible
stories and fairy tales that your Mother tells you. My
older grandchildren have been taken away to serve Japan
and you two little ones are all I have to count on."
Grandfather shut his eyes. He lifted his arm out from

35

under the covers and touched his hair as if to soothe his aching head.

Mother came to him and taking his hand, said, "What is it, Father? What is it you want?"

"Tell my grandchildren about our family while I can still hear. Show them some pictures of long ago. It will please me to hear you tell them about our family."

Mother went to her room and came back with a little wooden box. "Children," she said, "come over here by the light so we can look at these old pictures." The light was no better there, but we knew that she wanted to sit where she could best keep an eye on Grandfather. As soon as he fell asleep, I knew Mother would stop talking and we would have to leave the room so that he could rest. Down in front of us, she placed the wooden box. I had never seen it before. Although it was charred around the edges, I could still see the inlaid mother of pearl and the beautiful white cranes and flowers that had been delicately carved into the sides.

Mother looked at the box in silence. Then she stared off into the distance. Finally, she shook her head as if to chase away some horrible thoughts. "I had always hoped and prayed that I would be able to show you these pictures when we were free and happy. These pictures hold some of my happiest memories. But the stories I have to tell you . . ." She opened the box and, one by one, she showed us the pictures. First she showed us a picture of a tall man in a long flowing gown and a tall black hat; on his shoulder was a large multicolored bird with a long tail.

Mother said it was a picture of Grandfather when he was young. "Oh, how handsome he looks," I exclaimed as Inchun frowned at my excitement.

"Your Grandfather was a very important scholar. He passed all the government examinations. The bird was a present from one of his friends from China who had come to visit him." Then Mother said wistfully, "Under that special hat, your grandfather's hair was drawn into a small bun, called a topknot, on the top of his head. But when the Japanese occupied Korea, they gathered all the scholars in the town square and cut their topknots off. It was only hair," she continued, "but to your grandfather and the other proud scholars, it was a symbol of their culture and identity." The Japanese wanted all Koreans to dress like them and speak only their language. Everything Korean was forbidden.

Next Mother showed us a picture of their beautiful house. Then there was a very old picture of my grandmother holding my mother in her lap while her two young sons stood beside her. "Not long after they cut off Grandfather's topknot," she said, "they set fire to our village. My mother and my two older brothers died that night in the fire. Many people died. Your grandfather and I were among the few survivors. We escaped to Manchuria." I was getting confused. I wanted to ask why they had gone all the way to China, but Mother looked so sad that I kept silent.

Mother looked over at Grandfather, who now seemed to have fallen asleep. She seemed relieved, and quietly shut the picture box. We wanted to see and hear more, but we understood and began to tiptoe toward the door. But then Grandfather opened his eyes and looked at us. He wanted us to stay. We sat down again, and Mother reopened the box. She took out another picture and said, "This was the print shop in Manchuria where your father, grandfather, and I worked to publish a newspaper in *Hangul*. Your grandfather had been active in the Korean independence movement. Since it was dangerous for us to stay in Korea, we fled to Manchuria where we knew there was a large Korean community, and some under-ground activity. That was where I met your father. He was setting up a *Hangul* newspaper when your grandfather and I arrived." She pulled out a picture of a couple dressed in Chinese outfits, flanked by several other Chinese couples. I looked more closely at the couple in the middle, and saw that it was Mother and Father. "This is a picture of our wedding," she said. "We were married in Manchuria." She pointed to the woman next to her. "That is my dear friend Ling, who taught me to speak Chinese."

She showed us faded photographs of my sister, Theresa, and my three older brothers, Hanchun, Jaechun, and Hyunchun, with their Chinese neighbors. Everyone in our family had been born in China except for Inchun and me, I now realized. I peered into the box and saw a picture of Father Carroll, a Maryknoll priest whom I had once met. "I remember Father Carroll," I said. "He came here once when I was very little and gave me a book, but he never came again."

"Oh, my, do you really remember him?" Mother asked. "Yes," she added. "He came to say goodbye to us after the war began. He was one of the many American priests who were forced to leave Korea. He didn't want to leave us. He used to go from house to house at night and say Mass for us, since the Japanese forbade our going to church. But when the Japanese found out, they accused him of helping with the independence movement. He was a very important person in our lives . . . he baptized all of you children." I was glad that Inchun and I were finally included. I looked at Inchun, whose eyes darted from one picture to another. Mother continued to stare at the picture of Father Carroll, and I knew she missed him, especially now. I knew from my catechism lessons that old people needed some special blessing from a priest.

Mother continued as if she were anxious to be done with it. The determination in her eyes discouraged me from asking any more questions. "It was a hard life in Manchuria," she said haltingly, "but we were happy working for the independence movement. But not for long. The Japanese soon found us, and once again, in the middle of the night, they set fire to our homes. The soldiers, ready with their guns and swords, waited outside people's homes and shot them as they came running out of their burning houses. There were massacres in all the small

Korean settlements." I wasn't quite sure what the word *massacre* meant, but I didn't interrupt Mother as her eyes were filling with tears.

Mother continued. "I escaped with your three brothers and sister from Manchuria to Pyongyang with the help of Ling's family. Father and Grandfather stayed in Manchuria and hid in the basement of Ling's home waiting to set up the newspaper once again. Grandfather, however, was soon captured by the Japanese soldiers and tortured. After several months, Father and his friends managed to rescue Grandfather from the soldiers, and they sent him to Pyongyang disguised as a peasant. Well," she said, "you know what it's like in Pyongyang."

There were still so many things I wanted to know, and I wished she would continue. But she gathered the pictures together, and put them back in the box. "This box was all that was saved from those two fires." Mother looked pale and weak. She closed her eyes and shook her head. We looked at her in bewilderment. We had learned so much about our family; there had been so much we hadn't known. Why hadn't Mother and Grandfather told us before? Mother quietly took the box and went to sit by Grandfather's side.

Inchun and I went to my room, and we thought about what Mother had told us. I was glad to finally know my family's history, but I started to grow angry that Mother had kept it from me and Inchun for so long. We waited to be called again to Grandfather's room, when we heard Aunt Tiger mumbling to herself. "Poor Kisa asked Captain Narita three times. I knew what Narita would say. 'No doctors for the old dying Korean man. Doctors are busy helping the Imperial soldiers.' I expected as much." Aunt then saw us listening and stopped short. Was Grandfather really dying? I looked at Inchun. His face was dark, and he looked sad and lost as he stared at Aunt. Aunt looked at us, then hurried away.

Finally, Mother called us in again. Remembering what Aunt had said, we tiptoed in and Inchun grabbed my hand. To my great surprise, Grandfather opened his eyes and smiled. He lifted his fingers slightly as if to wave at us. We sat down close to him and waited. He looked us over from head to toe as if he wanted to memorize every little detail. He stretched out his hands. He wanted to touch our faces. We leaned toward him, and he touched my cheek with one hand and Inchun's with the other. His skin was cool and dry. He gazed at us for a while and then took our hands.

As Grandfather enveloped our hands in his, I felt a strange sensation. I felt as though a quiet, but peaceful, little Buddha had slowly crept inside me. Grandfather smiled, and let go of our hands. He closed his eyes again. I looked at Inchun. His dark eyes that had smiled as Grandfather held us were now filled with tears. I hugged him. I wanted him to feel the peaceful little Buddha that I had felt inside me a minute ago.

The next day we did not see Grandfather. We were not called into his room. Nobody had time for us. Inchun and I spent most of the day in the yard. While I was brooding with fear and sadness, Inchun hunched over his little corner of the yard, working on a picture. He drew in the dirt with a stick Grandfather had whittled for him, and he erased by sweeping the dirt with the small brush Mother had given him. He was drawing a picture of a Buddhist temple tucked away in the mountains. There were lots of monks wandering about, and animals were hiding in the mountains. I joined him and drew flowers: wild lilies, azaleas, little violets, and roses.

As we sat playing in the yard, a Buddhist monk entered through the gate dressed like a peasant in rough gray cotton. I knew he was bringing special herbs for Grandfather. The hours passed slowly, and still we had no news about Grandfather. Mother and Aunt Tiger were too busy taking care of him, and so we just waited. Finally, Aunt Tiger came and said that Grandfather wanted to see us again. She gave me a special dish of lemon oil and a little bit of soft gauze with which to rub his hands and his parched lips. As usual, Inchun was right behind me like my shadow. Grandfather's room was very dark and the air was somehow different. Mother looked at us as we came in, but remained motionless by Grandfather's side. Inchun and I went and sat near him, but Mother motioned for us to move even closer.

I started to rub a bit of cool lemon oil on his forehead. His breathing was very heavy and low, and he did not open his eyes. His face had taken on a bluish quality. But then a faint smile allayed my fears. He said with his eyes closed, "Will you rub some of that oil on my feet?" So relieved to hear his voice, I said, "Yes, Grandfather," as I picked up the bowl of lemon oil.

But Mother shot up like an arrow, lunged at the bowl of lemon oil and snatched it from me. "You and Inchun go outside," she said. "I will do that."

Grandfather's voice was weak, but he whispered with determination, "My daughter, did you not hear me ask my grandchildren, not you, to do it this time . . . It won't hurt them."

I had never seen Mother behave like that. She frightened me. Mother was quiet for a long time. I didn't understand. Inchun and I stared at the floor. After a long, uncomfortable silence, Mother gently handed me back the bowl and the white gauze. Mother did not always obey Grandfather, but I was glad she listened now.

She lifted the soft, white cotton blanket that covered Grandfather's feet. She took off his white socks as if she were unwrapping a precious object. After folding the blanket around his ankles to protect him from the draft, she stepped away. It was my turn to take over. I put the cloth into the bowl and squeezed it gently. I felt so privileged to be allowed to take care of Grandfather. I had never seen his bare feet before. They were always covered with white socks.

His feet were long and bony. They felt cool to the touch. I could see the veins, which seemed to form a road map down to his toes. But his toes were very strange. The tips of his toes were all wrinkled and looked like some little girl had practiced her sewing on them. He had no toenails. I knew he had no fingernails on his right hand, and I always thought he had hurt himself whittling. But no toenails! At first, I thought it strange, but then it occurred to me.

Sadness washed over me like a big ocean tide. My fingers trembled as I went over each toe with lemon oil. My head started to throb as all the horrible stories I had heard of Japanese cruelty went rushing through my mind. I held his toes in my hands. My eyes filled with tears. I wished that I could comfort these poor toes. I looked at Mother, who stood behind me clutching his socks, with tears in her eyes. I wanted her to send me outside. I couldn't look at his toes anymore. She saw my fumbling fingers and took the gauze from me. She dried his feet and covered them with the blanket. Grandfather lay motionless, his eyes closed. But I knew he was not asleep because I heard him swallow his sorrow. Inchun sobbed, "Grandfather, do they hurt?" "No, not anymore," Grandfather replied. "I am well now." Mother drew close to me and whispered, "Grandfather must rest now." Inchun sobbed as he followed me out.

Grandfather died soon after we left him. He died three days after Haiwon's birthday; three days after his beloved pine tree was chopped down.

I felt like a different person. I felt so many conflicting emotions struggling within me. The world seemed empty. The air was so dark and heavy, I could hardly breathe. I wanted to be peaceful like Grandfather. Mother, who had always told me that all would be well, that God would make sure of it, was not there. She sat in the corner of her dark room holding her Bible.

Aunt Tiger was busy taking care of little Inchun, who cried inconsolably. Whatever calmness he had shown had abandoned him now that Grandfather was dead. He developed a fever and would not eat anything. There was no way to distract him; he did not want to draw, spin his top, or follow me around the yard. He stayed in bed, hot and weak.

I went to Grandfather's room, sat in front of his scholar's desk and opened its many drawers. Everything looked empty and meaningless. The oxtail brushes didn't seem so special anymore. I didn't want to look at any of these things. They made me miss him too much. I was miserable and angry. If it were not for Captain Narita and his men, my grandfather would be alive and would be with me now.

I went back to my room. I cried because I missed Grandfather. I cried because I felt so alone and scared and full of hatred for Captain Narita and those Japanese soldiers. Feeling weak, I went out to the yard and sat on the stump of the pine tree. I tried to remember all that Grandfather had taught me. I thought of his whittling, his brush writing, his meditating, and then I thought of his last peaceful smile. Hadn't I felt that special little Buddha when he held my hand in his? As soon as I thought of his peaceful face and the cool touch of his hand and that little chuckling Buddha, my anger, frustration, fear, and utter loneliness began to subside.

The stump of the pine tree felt cool against me. I rubbed my leg against the stump and felt the roughness of the bark. Then, I centered myself on the stump and crossed my legs. I wanted to meditate like Grandfather. I closed my eyes tight. I just had to see that little chuckling Buddha again, and I began to rub my eyes. I started to see stars bursting beneath my eyelids, but no little Buddha. Instead, warm tears welled up.

Slowly, a feeling of calmness came over me. I dried my tears and looked up at the evening sky. A small, faint star was shining in the distance. I felt as though I had been immersed in a cool sea, and the red flames of pain and bitterness had been extinguished. I thought the Buddha's spirit was inside of me. Suddenly, I understood what Grandfather meant when he said, "One's life is short, but the life of the spirit is long." The Buddha brought me a little bit of Grandfather's spirit and Grandfather's peace. I thought of his lessons on Um and Yang — darkness and light, pain and joy, evil and good. Grandfather told me that all these tensions and conflicts were necessary in the struggle for perfect harmony.

Harmony. That was the word he used. "Harmony will prevail," he used to say. "After darkness, there will be light. The light cannot come without the darkness. Better days are bound to come now." I got up and went to Mother's room. She sat there rigidly like a statue. Were it not for her tears, I would have been afraid that she too had died. I wanted to tell her that all would be well. But I did not know how. I just stood next to her and leaned against her shivering body as hot, silent tears streamed down my cheeks.

Chapter Four

It had been several days since Mother had even spoken.
Her pale lips were tightly pursed and her eyes avoided ours
as if she were trying to contain a sorrow that would otherwise come gushing forth. She worked frantically on what
Aunt brought her. Could such activity make the pain disappear?

"Mother, why don't you come out and show me how to
sew socks fast, as you do?" I asked. But she would not
answer or even look up from her work. When Inchun
went over to her and whined playfully, "Mother, look at
the strange way *Nuna* combed my hair," she didn't even
crack a smile. She simply ordered me to fix his hair prop-
erly. All day long, she sat there in her dimly lit room, her
eyes glued to her needlework. When the sock girls came
in the morning, she didn't come to greet them. And
when they left, looking exhausted, she had no kind
words to offer. She did not seem to notice what went on
around her. She seemed like a lost ghost. She did not
mention Grandfather. I felt that she too was lost to me. I
was afraid her spirit had gone away with Grandfather's. I

longed to see her smile and to hear her tell us that everything would be all right.

Aunt Tiger was busy trying to cover for Mother at the sock factory, and Inchun and I did what we could. Sitting on the ground by the tree stump, we sorted, folded, and then packed into bundles of twelve, or "*tah,*" the pile of ugly green socks that Aunt Tiger put out for us in the morning. There was no time to be lost. The sock girls rushed in, anxious to meet their daily quota. Haiwon came extra early as always and whispered to us, "Do you think she will come out and talk to us today?" I lowered my head in silence. I didn't know the answer. Then, Okja came running in and, to cheer us up, poked us in the sides. "Did you sleep well, little ones?" she asked. "My, how quiet we all are!" Then she gently nudged us and tried to topple us over. With her long bony fingers, she tapped on our heads and said, "What deep thoughts are traveling through these two clever heads? No talking today either, huh? Not even a small smile, eh? Haven't seen your dimples for days. Come on, smile and show me your dimples. Your mother walks around like a ghost and you little ones have lost your tongues. What a dreadfully quiet house. Where is your Aunt Tiger, the talking machine?" Okja then rushed off with the others into the factory shaking her head. I couldn't say anything to Okja or Haiwon. But I was glad that they stopped and talked to us, even if it was only for a minute.

As we kept folding the socks and bundling them into *tah,* I kept thinking about Mother. The Buddha probably knew how much Grandfather loved Mother. Maybe the Buddha had taken Mother's soul to keep Grandfather company. But what about Inchun and me? Why were we left behind? I couldn't help thinking that the Buddha or Mother's God was punishing me for the hatred I felt for Captain Narita. I felt guilty and afraid.

As I sat thinking, Inchun glared at me and said, "*Nuna,* how many pairs are there in one *tah?*"

Startled and annoyed, I retorted, "Twelve, of course."

"Well then, why does this bundle have eleven pairs, and this one fifteen pairs?" he asked. It was a good thing he was paying attention. We all would have been in trouble with the Japanese police and the merchants when they came to collect the finished goods. Mother was no longer around to check everything, and without her, we were more nervous than ever that the Japanese would not be happy with our work.

Embarrassed by my mistakes, I started to rebundle them, and tears began to roll down my cheeks. I tried to hide them from Inchun. He shouldn't see his big sister cry. But I soon saw that he too had tears in his eyes and he tried to rub them away with his little fingers, which were dirty and scratched from the burlap twine used to tie the bundles of socks.

Aunt Tiger brought us more socks and said, "Captain Narita still has not paid us or the girls. I must go and ask him to pay us or, better yet, to pay us with rice. Those Japanese rice merchants are getting whatever price they want from us hungry Koreans." I was glad she was with us

50

and that she talked constantly. It was soothing to hear a grown-up talk. It broke the heavy silence that weighed upon us.

Aunt Tiger must have noticed that we had been crying. "Give your mother some time," she told us. "She will be back to normal soon. I just wish that she could make a visit to the convent and talk to your sister, Theresa. If only Father Carroll were still around! Oh, where are the Americans? Not even one American priest is here in Pyongyang now. They've all abandoned us. Well, it isn't their fault; what could they do? They were all chased out by the Japanese after the war began. Their churches were closed and they were accused of insulting the Heavenly Emperor and of being the White Devils' spies . . . I heard they were shipped to Africa, then to America after that. I hope they are safe in their own land . . . at least they're free of the Japanese soldiers." Aunt Tiger went on and on. She didn't seem to care whether anyone heard her or not. Maybe she knew that it made us feel better just to hear her voice.

Later that morning, Captain Narita came by for a second inspection. He said he wanted to make sure that we were all working as hard as we could to serve "the ever-victorious Japanese army and the Heavenly Emperor." Every time he and his lieutenants marched in to inspect our work, chills went through me. He walked by Inchun and me and went into the factory. It was unusual for him to come twice in one morning, and we were relieved when he and his lieutenants left looking fairly satisfied.

But the following morning, Captain Narita came back, and instead of making the routine inspection of the factory, he ordered Aunt Tiger to get Mother. Aunt Tiger rushed inside, and they both came running out.

Captain Narita gazed calmly at Mother as he stroked his mustache that twitched as he formed his icy smile. He spoke very slowly in a hushed tone. We could barely hear him, and even Mother cocked her head slightly to hear. "Your sock girls did not do good work this week. We Imperial soldiers can put them to better use. Our victorious Imperial soldiers need to be rewarded for their heroic achievements on the battlefields. Our great Heavenly Emperor will be pleased to know that your girls volunteered to help our soldiers fight better. Your girls will be honored to bring glory to the Emperor."

I did not know what that meant, but I saw a look of horror come over Mother's face. With a deep bow Mother said, "Most honorable Imperial Captain, it was my fault that productivity went down. I was not able to work fast enough after the loss of my father. Please do not take the sock girls away . . ." She trembled as she spoke.

Her face was pale and her eyes were filled with tears. I could not believe that she was bowing so humbly and desperately before this cruel little man. She seemed willing to do almost anything to change his mind. "Please let them be . . . give us another chance. I will see to it that the Imperial police are pleased with our sock production. We will please the Heavenly Emperor with more work." I wished I knew what they were talking about. I did not understand why Mother was so frightened. "Most honorable Imperial Captain, please, please . . . ," she said over and over again. With great satisfaction, Captain Narita stroked the edges of his stubby mustache and adjusted his sword belt about his thin waist. He surveyed the yard, lost in his own thoughts. Then he and his lieutenants departed without a word.

We stood listening to the sound of their swords clanking against their guns as they walked away. I was amazed at how this scrawny little man could inspire such fear in my mother with just a few words. I watched Mother's ghostly face as she stared after Captain Narita. She stood motionless and kept looking at the gate as if she were still waiting and praying for him to return with an answer.

I had always had a vague notion that something horrible might happen if the girls did not produce enough socks, but I was never sure what it might be. Aunt Tiger was silently gnawing on her lower lip and furiously tying the socks in bundles. She kept looking over at Mother, who was pacing back and forth.

Mother wrung her hands and trembled. She mumbled under her breath like a crazy person. I knew this was not a time to ask questions. Even Aunt Tiger was silent.

All of a sudden, Okja came running out into the yard. I was surprised to see her, for none of the girls ever left their machines during the day except for lunch. She stared at Mother in silent terror. Whether or not Captain

Narita walked into the factory, the girls somehow always knew when he had come by the house.

Mother looked at Okja, but her mind was elsewhere. After what seemed like a long time, she said, "Captain Narita has threatened to take you girls away. He said you did not produce enough socks, but you cannot possibly do any more! I should have been out here with you. What am I going to do, Okja? I better tell the girls . . . I want you to hide. I don't want any of you to come here anymore."

Okja's eyes filled with tears, but she bit her lip to keep from crying. "There is no place for us to hide," she said quietly. "He knows where we live and whom we know, and if he wants to, he'll find us and take us to the front. No matter where we go, we are their prisoners. It'll do no good to hide. He'll only make you suffer more for letting us go. All we can do is work day and night to produce more socks and hope he'll change his mind."

Haiwon came running out into the yard, wiping the sweat from her brow. Squinting in the bright sunlight, she said, "The girls are saying something is terribly wrong. We want to know what's going on. We know the rat was here talking to you. How come he did not inspect the factory? What did he want?" Haiwon looked at Mother and Okja. Suddenly she started wailing, "Oh, no, not that, not that, oh no . . . I wish I were dead, I wish I were dead!" and she fell to her knees crying, pounding on her chest with her fists.

Mother and Okja dropped to the ground and embraced her, steadying her hands and wiping her tears. "Come. Let's go into the sock factory and talk about this and see what we can do," said Mother.

When I got up to follow them, Aunt Tiger grabbed me and kept me with her. I watched as the three of them entered the ugly barrack. I heard the machines go off. There was silence, then violent cries of anguish. It grew quiet again. What were they talking about? I waited. Soon the machines started up again, and I saw Mother come stumbling out. She was drenched with perspiration. She stood listlessly outside the barrack clutching the door handle.

Aunt Tiger rushed to her side and led her to the straw mat where we were sitting. "They are so brave," said Mother to Aunt Tiger. "They want to try to make even more socks in the hope that Narita will change his mind. But I wish they would just try to hide. I don't want them to come back here. I can't bear to see them taken away. I don't care what Narita does to me."

Aunt Tiger looked at Mother in disbelief. "You must be mad with fever! You know Captain Narita better than that by now! Okja is right. They have nowhere to hide. They all know that if even one of them doesn't come to work, they will all suffer for it. We all will. There's no escape for us. We are like mice trapped in a dungeon of wildcats. We are Koreans; we are a cursed race and there is no hope for us as long as the Japanese are around."

Mother didn't seem to be listening. With her fists clenched, she stared at the barrack, praying for a revelation to save her dear sock girls.

Aunt Tiger continued. "They use us, they toy with us, and eventually they'll kill us all, one way or another. Our lives are worth no more than a fly's. 'A voluntary offering for the glory of the Emperor' . . . How skillfully they lie, lie, lie! Those girls would rather die than be 'spirit girls' for the Emperor's soldiers. When I think of how many truckloads of girls they've taken to the front already . . . I heard half of them killed themselves by jumping off the speeding trucks rather than be locked in those latrines and used by those soldiers. Our poor girls!" Aunt Tiger was raving like a mad woman.

Mother suddenly seemed to have realized what Aunt Tiger was saying and whispered harshly, "Please, please stop! The children!" With her fists still clenched, she continued pacing up and down the length of the yard, staring at the sock factory. I wished they would tell me what was happening. What did "spirit girls" mean? Why were they being sent to the front?

I was terribly afraid for the sock girls and yet I didn't even know why. But I was somehow relieved to see Mother up and about. I had been so worried that she would die of grief, crying day after day in her dark room. Within an hour of Captain Narita's visit, she had resumed her duties and was rushing about, overseeing production. Fear and helplessness had been transformed into desperate determination.

The next day Mother got up long before the sun and had Kisa inspect and grease all the machines. The girls came earlier than ever and immediately started working. They had all resolved to do the impossible; they would increase production and make Captain Narita change his mind. For several days, Mother and the girls worked from the crack of dawn until late at night, without even taking a break at mealtimes. Inchun and I busily folded and bundled the socks to keep pace with them.

Mother looked more and more frail. Her face had become flushed with fever. I noticed Aunt Tiger glancing at her with grave concern. One night, as we were finishing up for the day, I heard Aunt Tiger say to her, "You are working like a crazy person. You're making yourself sick, and it won't do any good. The Japanese have been taking our girls for years. We all knew it was only a matter of time." She tried to convince Mother to get some sleep or at least to eat something. I wished Mother would listen to her, but she said nothing and continued to work. Even Inchun and I kept folding socks and mending stitches, working late into the night by candlelight.

Each day Mother waited expectantly for Captain Narita. The Japanese merchants and the police came by to collect the socks and seemed very pleased, but we waited anxiously for Captain Narita's decision. We just kept working, but I could sense that with each passing day, Mother and Aunt Tiger were growing more and more apprehensive. One morning as we worked on in the stagnant heat, Mother said, "I never thought I would say this, but I wish Captain Narita would come by. We need to know if there is any hope. They've been working so hard, and we haven't been paid in weeks now. We'll all go hungry soon. If he doesn't come by tomorrow morning, maybe I'll go to his office and see if those awful guards will let me see him."

Late that night, I watched the dim lights go off in the factory. I didn't go out to the yard to wave good night to the girls. I wanted to be by myself in Grandfather's room. I was tired of working so hard. How long would we have to live like this? When would Grandfather's merciful Buddha or Mother's Catholic God come to help us? As I sat in Grandfather's room trying to recapture his warmth and calm, I looked out and watched the sock girls talking, shaking the day's dust from their hair and clothes, and stretching their weary arms and legs. Some were busily opening and closing their hands to stretch their stiff fingers. Others rubbed their eyes and wiped their tongues with their handkerchiefs to rid themselves of the dust and lint. They exchanged a few words with each other and with Kisa, and then headed toward the gate. "It's starting to rain. Be careful," I heard Mother say. Although exhausted, they all wore a look of liberation as they stared up at the dark rainy sky. They had gotten through another day.

Suddenly, the gate burst open. Everyone froze in horror. Two soldiers stood behind Captain Narita with their guns slung over their shoulders. One of them held a large black umbrella over Captain Narita to protect him from the rain. Through the open gate, I saw a big truck parked outside. I heard Mother moan helplessly, "Oh, Lord, Oh, Lord . . . Merciful Lord . . . "

The dark sky broke loose with a crack of thunder and a bolt of lightning. It started to pour. How I wished a huge thunderbolt would strike right where Captain Narita and the soldiers stood. Oblivious of the torrential downpour, the girls started sobbing. "I wish I were dead, I wish I were dead," I heard several of them whimper. They clutched one another in desperation. Huddled together in the pouring rain, they looked like helpless animals. I wished that just this once, I could run out and beat up Captain Narita. But I couldn't move. I sat there watching with tears streaming down my face.

"You should all be very proud and honored that it is now your turn to serve Our Heavenly Emperor. You will give the soldiers the special spirit to fight harder against the White Devils," said Captain Narita cheerfully. "Our Heavenly Emperor will be happy that you volunteered to help the soldiers. Now get into the truck and get out of this rain." The two soldiers began to herd the girls toward the truck. Some screamed and fell to the muddy ground, but were jabbed with guns and forced onto the truck.

"Please do not take them . . . some of them are not even fifteen," Mother implored. "The older ones have babies and old grandparents at home to take care of." Captain Narita smiled for an instant, showing a row of crooked teeth, and then motioned for his lieutenants to hurry as he looked up at the black sky.

I saw Haiwon being pushed toward the truck. I heard her cry just as she had on her birthday. Only this time, her cry was more faint, as though she could not even muster the courage to go on any longer.

I saw Okja spit at the soldier who was jabbing her in the ribs with his gun as he tried to get her onto the truck. The angry soldier lifted his gun to hit her. Like lightning, Kisa shot out from nowhere and kept the soldier from hitting her. The soldier dealt a blow to Kisa instead, who fell to the ground screaming. Okja tried to run to Kisa, but the soldier grabbed Okja and tossed her onto the truck like a dead cat. The other soldier kicked Kisa in the ribs. Kisa lay doubled over in the mud crying out to the girls. Captain Narita looked at him with disgust and shouted to the driver. The truck pulled away and sped off in the darkness of the storm. I knew better than to go outside. From the door of Grandfather's room, I saw my mother standing in the rain, wringing her hands.

Aunt Tiger brought Kisa inside and began bandaging his head. "What made you think you could fight the soldiers with their guns and swords?" Aunt Tiger said. "Haven't you seen enough . . . how they kill us like flies?" I sat down next to them, and I wanted to ask Aunt Tiger where the girls were being taken and what would happen to them. But I felt it was silly to ask. Wherever they were being taken, I could tell it was a fate even worse than death.

Kisa wept uncontrollably, and said, "I will never see those girls again . . . I couldn't save even one of them."

"It was only a matter of time," Aunt Tiger said. "You knew this day would come sooner or later."

"Maybe we will all see each other again. Maybe the war will end soon and they'll return to us," added Mother, as she came inside. When she saw me, she rushed over and held me tightly as if she wanted to squeeze all the fear out of me and said, "I'm sorry, I'm sorry, I'm sorry . . . We could truly use one miracle now, just one miracle." Mother's hot tears fell upon my forehead. Her voice was shaking and her body trembled. She was burning up with fever, and she shivered in her wet clothes. I touched her rough hands. All that frantic work had not done any good. It didn't matter how many socks they made. The Japanese could do whatever they wanted and no one could stop them.

From my bed, I heard the Lord's Prayer. I got up and peeked into Mother's room, and there, gathered around a candle and a small crucifix, were Mother, Aunt Tiger, and Kisa. Aunt Tiger was no longer making fun of Mother's Catholic God. I fell asleep as I listened to their devout prayers against the drumming of the rain. Kisa's voice was soothing, and I pretended that his voice was that of my father, three brothers, and my grandfather.

I must have fallen asleep. I felt a hot breeze brush against me, and then strange noises coming from the yard. I lay still in my bed. I could smell the candle that had been burning. I heard whispering in the next room. I got up and saw three figures, peering out at the yard through a crack in the rice-paper paneled doors. They were looking across the yard at the sock factory. I went over and saw that the lights were all on in the sock factory. For a split second I thought Mother's miracle had happened and the soldiers had brought the girls back to make some more socks. "Mother, are the sock girls back?" "Shhh," she replied. "Sit with us and be quiet. The soldiers are taking the machines and loading them onto the truck. They're probably taking them to be made into more weapons."

I rubbed my eyes and looked out. Several uniformed police had dismantled the machines, and were taking them from the sock factory and loading them onto the truck parked outside. "Those are not even theirs to take," said Kisa. "Those are ours . . . We bought them with our hard-earned money from the Japanese merchants, who probably stole them from other Koreans!"

Mother was quiet. "Since when does ownership matter to the Japanese?" said Aunt Tiger. "They take whatever they need from us. What good are those machines to us now? I had hoped we could trade them in for some rice, but that was silly of me. Let the bastards take them all. What else can we do?"

I was glad to see the machines go. It would be too sad to look at them day after day. Too much had happened today. Soon the rain stopped and there was a cool breeze. I looked out at the stump of the pine tree and the empty sock factory. The front gate was wide open and swinging in the wind. No one bothered to close it. What was the sense? Those gates provided no privacy or security. I wished I had slept through the night. The grown-ups were relieved that we were safe and only prayed that things would not get any worse.

I sat in helpless silence and watched the dawn break. The sun rose like any other day. It shone brightly, as if it knew nothing of our sadness. I felt the bright sun was heartless and cruel to shine so derisively, and I shut my eyes in defiance.

Chapter Five

Early one morning, Mother received a notice from one of Captain Narita's lieutenants. She stared at it blankly, and then put it in her pocket. I wondered what it meant. What more could they do to us? She looked over at me, and sighed. "They say you must learn to be a loyal and obedient subject and work to bring victory in the war. We have to enroll you in the Japanese school tomorrow," she said. I knew Mother had hoped the war would end before Inchun and I had to go to the Japanese school.

The next morning, Mother prepared my lunch box for the first day of school. There was a little piece of egg next to some sweet black beans and a small scoop of glistening white rice. We usually ate porridge made from barley and millet, and I knew Mother must have been saving this white rice for a special occasion. It looked so delicious, and she had packed it in a beautiful wooden lunch box that Grandfather had carved a long time ago. It was a rectangular box made of pine, with a sliding top. On one side of the box was a groove in which a pair of wooden chopsticks was cleverly concealed. I pulled out the chopsticks and saw that there were rosebuds carved on them. The lunch box felt smooth and warm in my hands. Mother had gone to so much trouble for me.

"Aunt Tiger will take you to school," Mother told me as she mustered a smile. "Just be very quiet and attentive and do as they tell you. Say, '*Hai, Sensei!*' (meaning 'Yes, Teacher') and you will be fine." The smile could hardly be sustained on her pale and feverish features. I tried to look happy about meeting some children my own age. I didn't want Mother to worry; I knew she was afraid for me.

Little Inchun stood quietly holding Mother's hand. He looked at me with great concern and said, "*Nuna*, remember not to speak one word of Korean and don't ask any questions. Just be quiet like me." I was startled to hear such wise advice from little Inchun. But I nodded, and smiled. He looked particularly pale and skinny that morning, but there was still that gentle twinkle in his big dark eyes. I thought of how Mother had always said that there was a wise old man living inside her little boy. I remembered how he always followed me like my silent little shadow. This would be the first time that we would be apart all day long, and I was sure that he would feel lost without me.

Aunt Tiger pulled me by the hand and rushed me out the door. "The Imperial police even took our clock," she muttered. "Everything we had has been melted down to make more weapons. 'What do Koreans need a clock for? They can guess by looking at the sun' . . . We better get going or we might be late for your first day."

The streets were quiet. We saw several students in their worn gray uniforms. As we approached the building, I felt more and more confused. I kept telling myself I could handle whatever they did to me, and I would do just as Mother said and say "*Hai, Sensei!*" no matter what. Most of all, I had to remember not to speak a word of Korean. I remembered how my older brother, Hyunchun, had come running home one day two years before, his forehead dripping with blood. As Mother held him and applied the bandage, Hyunchun told us through his tears, "I asked for a pencil in Korean and the teacher hit me with a metal ruler." I struggled to put this out of my mind, and tried to think of how nice it would be to make some friends my own age. Maybe I would make a friend that day. I could show her my pretty lunch box.

Aunt Tiger was unusually quiet. "Do you know who will teach me?" I asked.

"Yes, I think it will be Narita Sensei." My eyes opened wide with terror, and I stopped. The thought of seeing anyone having to do with Captain Narita sent shivers through me. "Yes," she said, "she is Captain Narita's wife and she has been teaching the first grade for many years." I said nothing. I was too frightened. She tried to comfort me. "I know her. Maybe I can see her and I'll tell her that you're my niece." We turned off the main street of Kirimni and walked down a long narrow road. "We have to speak Japanese now. People might hear us," she whispered. Now I really did not want to go. I could understand Japanese, but I had never spoken a word of it, and I

66

didn't want to. I squeezed Aunt Tiger's hand and she squeezed mine back.

I thought of the chuckling Buddha that I had seen when I was at Grandfather's bedside; the little Buddha had made me feel happier when I had been so worried about Grandfather. I needed to see this happy little Buddha again, and so I closed my eyes and rubbed them hard. I saw stars of many different colors, but I could not see the chuckling Buddha. I kept rubbing and rubbing my eyes. Suddenly, I saw a huge stone Buddha come falling through the starry skies. With a great crash, it landed right in front of me. I stared at the stone statue sitting so serenely. He looked like Grandfather. The other students in the street began to shout with glee and gather around the statue. The Japanese police and Captain Narita came running over and shouted at us. They tried to move the statue, but it would not budge. The students clapped their hands and began rolling with laughter as they watched the Imperial police struggle fruitlessly. The police mumbled and yelled. They looked at each other, then at the students, and finally, broke into laughter. They laughed and laughed. They took off their swords and guns and threw them by the side of the road.

Aunt Tiger shook me and said, "What's the matter? Come on, we have to keep going. What's that strange smile on your face? Why are you walking with your eyes closed like that? Do you feel all right?" I nodded my head and opened my eyes. I was sad that I could not continue my daydream, but I felt better. "I tell you, in all my days,

I have never met two more unusual children than you and your little brother. Did you hear the advice that Inchun gave you? What a little old man! One minute you two are daydreaming children, and the next, you're wise old adults. I don't know what to make of you two anymore."

Up ahead loomed the big gray schoolhouse. High stone walls surrounded the building, and the gate was half closed. Aunt Tiger asked the guard if she could stay and speak to Narita Sensei. The uniformed guard laughed heartily. "You Korean peasant! You want to speak to our Imperial teacher!" Aunt Tiger's face turned red and she shouted in Korean, "Imperial teacher, haa! Narita Sensei used to sell fish in Hokkaido." I pushed her away and begged her to go as I watched the guard's jaw muscles tighten with fury. Mumbling under her breath, Aunt Tiger left me.

The students were standing in a series of straight lines, the boys on one side of the school yard and the girls on the other. I looked around and slipped into the middle of the line of girls by the wall in front of the sign that said "First Grade." Lined up in size order from little to big they stood at attention like little soldiers. I was afraid to go to the front where I belonged, and no one said a word to me. Along one wall were piles and piles of sand bags. Neatly arranged along the other wall was a row of bamboo sticks with sharpened points.

One girl then turned to me and whispered in Japanese, "Is this your first day?" I nodded my head and must have looked confused. "You don't speak Japanese?" I nodded my head again. The girl mumbled in Korean, "You are a strange one." I was delighted to hear her speak Korean and my face must have lit up. Encouraged by my response, she introduced herself. "My name is Unhi. I'm warning you, this is the last time you'll hear me speak Korean. We'll get in trouble if Narita Sensei hears us. You never know if someone will tattle to the teacher. Anyway you'd better move to the front where all the midgets are." She gave me a little push.

The other girls who were mutely standing in line looked at Unhi with displeasure. Unhi ignored them. Though her manner was gruff, I knew I had made a friend. I did not even have a chance to tell her my name. When I went to the front, a girl grabbed me. "You are shorter than I am. Come here." She was delighted to find someone shorter than she was, and I suddenly found myself at the head of the line. I hated being the first in line and stood there trembling.

The main doors of the schoolhouse were just ahead of me, and I saw all the teachers coming out and walking toward us. There were some young ones as well as several older ones wearing gold-rimmed glasses. I was anxious to see which one was our teacher. There was suddenly complete silence in the yard, and then a skinny boy in a gray uniform that seemed too big for him marched to the center of the yard and shouted in Japanese, "Attention!" Everyone stiffened. He shouted another command, and everyone bowed from the waist. A short thin woman in a dark blue and white Japanese kimono with a cherry blossom print stood directly in front of me. Her hair was carefully arranged in a bun that looked like a large dough-nut sitting on top of her head. She looked me over from head to toe with disdain. I looked up at her before quickly forcing my gaze back to the ground. I knew they didn't like it when Koreans looked them in the eye. So this is Narita Sensei, I thought to myself. Her icy glare resembled her husband's, and she too wore gold-rimmed glasses.

The boy who had shouted the commands resumed his place in line. A thin older man mounted the podium in the center of the yard and shouted, "Face east." All the students turned to the right and faced a pedestal on which something sat shrouded by a curtain with a golden tassel. The man at the podium lifted a baton, and sud-denly the familiar Japanese national anthem, the "Kimigayo," came blaring over the loudspeaker. I knew the song by heart. I had learned it with my three older brothers after Hanchun had come back from his first day of school with bruises for not having known the words. I knew all the words, but I just mouthed them. I couldn't bring myself to speak the language of Captain Narita. Suddenly I realized Narita Sensei had bent down and put her ear next to my mouth. I tried to sing out, but I just couldn't. No sound would come forth. She glared at me, and the sun reflecting off her gold-rimmed glasses blinded me. I cleared my throat hoping it would help, but still no sound. I wished the song would stop, but it went on and on. Narita Sensei jabbed me in the side with the ruler hidden in the sleeve of her kimono. I started to cry.

I didn't know why I wasn't able to sing. I wanted to. I wanted to do whatever I was told just as Mother and Aunt Tiger had instructed me.

After the *"Kimigayo"* was finally over, a different boy went to the center of the yard. He shouted, "Attention!" Then he bowed to the man at the podium. All the other students did the same. The man at the podium was Principal Watanabe. He clapped his hands and then walked over to the shrine on the pedestal and pulled the gold rope ceremoniously. Everyone looked up reverently as the curtain parted. He performed this duty as if it were the most sacred and important thing in his life. The curtain was slowly opened and behind it was a small wooden shrine. He then opened the little door. The Japanese god's image was enshrined there, but we couldn't see anything. Everyone, including the teachers and the principal, stood at attention facing this shrine. We always faced east, for that was where the sun rises and the direction in which the Japanese Emperor's palace was situated in Japan.

Principal Watanabe clapped his hands and we all bowed. I still hoped to see what was in the shrine, and so I did not bow as deeply as I should have. Narita Sensei whacked me on the head with her ruler. "The Heavenly Emperor is too divine to be gazed upon by human eyes," she rasped. My face burned and I felt hot tears filling my eyes. The students began to recite the pledge that also was so familiar to me: "We the fortunate subjects of Imperial Japan pledge our undying loyalty and good wishes for the prosperity and good health of the Heavenly Emperor and his empire where the sun will never set. We wish for the victory of the heavenly Japanese soldiers and the defeat of the White Devils."

The curtain was slowly drawn shut and the *"Kimigayo"* played again as we marched to our respective rooms. My head hurt and my throat was dry from trying to swallow my tears. No one had ever hit me before. I wanted to go home. We stood in line for a long time, waiting for all the upperclassmen to file in to their classrooms first. Finally, Narita Sensei started walking, and the girl behind me nudged me to follow. We went into a clean classroom with a shiny wooden floor. We took off our shoes and arranged them neatly in the shelves by the door.

Like porcelain dolls, all the girls sat in their seats with their hands folded. They stared straight ahead at the blank chalkboard. There were no extra seats, so I quickly went to a corner and sat quietly on the floor hoping to stay out of trouble for the rest of the day. I had thought there might be a minute or two to chat and meet the other girls, but I was mistaken. Narita Sensei sat at her wooden desk and fussed about arranging her belongings. Then she took out her black book and surveyed the class. She motioned for me to come to her. *"Aoki Shizue,"* she said. I didn't say anything. That was not my name. I knew my brothers had Japanese names that they used at school, but at home we called them by their Korean names or Christian baptismal names. To me, they were just *"oppa,"* which meant "older brother." I knew our last name was

"Aoki" in Japanese, but I was not used to "Shizue." I stood before her, feeling confused and afraid.

Narita Sensei banged her ruler on her desk, which sent a pencil flying. It hit me in the eye and I started to cry. I wished she would let me go and sit down. Instead, she shouted, "You refuse to talk to your Sensei?" Unhi rushed up and said something to Sensei. This made Sensei even angrier. She pounded on her desk, and motioned for Unhi to sit down. I learned that the worst thing one could do was to speak up for your friend. We were to mind our own business at all times. Narita Sensei resumed the class. Everyone's name was called. Mine was called again and I answered as all the other children had by saying, "Hai, Sensei" and raising my right hand. I knew I had no choice. My baptismal name and my Korean name would be used only at home from now on. Here I would have to answer to this strange Japanese name; I was someone I did not want to be and I had to pretend.

We then had to sing the "Kimigayo" all over again and pledge our undying devotion to the Emperor. I was relieved that I had learned the pledge, for Narita Sensei was watching me carefully. I did not want to get my family in trouble. I knew that if I did not behave, they might cut our rice ration or do something worse. Captain Narita knew exactly how best to punish us. I thought of how pale my mother looked that morning, and how skinny Inchun looked. They couldn't take much more.

Finally, it was time to sit down and open our notebooks.

I went back to my place on the floor. I wanted only to stay out of Narita Sensei's sight. Sensei put up two poster-boards. One was a picture of two Japanese pilots standing in front of a shiny airplane with Japanese flags painted on the wings. The other was a picture of two tall American soldiers in green fatigues, their faces painted black. Their planes were dirty and dilapidated. Narita Sensei pointed to the Japanese soldiers and had us repeat after her, "*Hikoki, hikoki, gawai hikoki,*" which meant, "Airplane, airplane, pretty airplane." Then, pointing to the other picture, she said, "The White Devils are losing the war. See how funny they look." She laughed and the children imitated her. She moved her pointer back and forth from one picture to the other, and I watched the children reciting these chants over and over as if they were familiar old songs. Narita Sensei smiled. "Well done, children," she said.

One by one she called on every child to come up to the front of the classroom and lead the recitation. Unhi went first. She did exactly as she was told and the class repeated after her, and then the next girl went up. I looked at them in astonishment. How could they repeat these ridiculous slogans so easily? I felt sorry for them, and I wondered if these little girls really believed what they were saying. I was glad that I knew something about America.

There was no break from these tedious recitations. I wanted to go to the bathroom, but did not dare attract attention. As I was out of her line of vision, Narita Sensei seemed to have forgotten me. I was grateful to be left alone; I didn't care that I didn't have a desk or chair. As I listened to Narita Sensei's shrill voice, I looked around. I saw one girl wiggling in her chair. Pretty soon, a little puddle formed beneath her. I looked around the room and counted four other little puddles. I looked up at their faces and saw them continuing to recite their lessons as if nothing were wrong. I couldn't wait much longer myself and I sat squeezing my legs together hoping that I could manage to wait until she let us out.

Narita Sensei called on yet another girl to come up to the front of the room and lead the recitation. The girl had wet her pants. She was ashamed, and just sat in her chair, looking nervous and frightened. Narita Sensei whacked her ruler against the side of her desk and shouted at the girl to come up to the board. The girl stood up. The back of her skirt was dripping wet. Narita Sensei looked at her in disgust and asked the whole class to take out their cleaning bags. Each girl had a little bag with some rags and some polishing wax. The children started to push all the chairs and tables back to one side of the classroom, and got on their hands and knees to wax the whole floor. It all seemed very routine to them. No one spoke. Those who had wet their pants seemed relieved to clean up the little puddles they had made.

I stood and watched. She made us all feel worthless and ashamed of ourselves. Unhi saw me and quickly tossed me a rag and part of her stick of wax. We crawled about the floor polishing it as best we could. When we finished, the girls arranged all the desks and chairs, and put their rags and sticks of wax neatly in their desks. They sat quietly and waited for Narita Sensei to continue with the lessons. I was amazed at their efficiency. I knew that this would soon become routine for me, too.

I took my place on the floor. After a long while, Narita Sensei looked up at the class and said with a big smile, "You Koreans are so good at following orders. You are lucky that the Japanese soldiers are here to protect you from the White Devils, aren't you?" "*Hai, Sensei!*" the children shouted in unison. "Remember your happiness depends on the victory of the Imperial soldiers," she said as the bell rang. Our hands were dirty and caked with wax, but we sat and ate our lunches in silence. I tried to take out the splinter in my finger. Then like the others, I started eating my lunch.

Narita Sensei left the room and an older girl came in to watch us. I looked over at the little girl who had put me at the head of the line. She had been one of the girls who had wet her pants. I felt sorry for her. I noticed she had no lunch box. All she had to eat were two little rice balls sprinkled with salt. I pushed my lunch box over toward her. There were still some beans left, and a bit of egg. It smelled so good because Mother had cooked with a little bit of sesame oil, and I knew the little girl would like some. The big girl saw me sharing my lunch, and immediately took it away. She walked out with it, and that was the last time I saw the beautiful lunch box that Grandfather had made. Later Unhi grabbed me and said, "Mind your own business. Never help any of the other girls in the class. It's a bad thing to do. Just take care of yourself."

After lunch, the whole school gathered in the yard. The June sun was hot, but I was glad to be out of that classroom. We were given big burlap bags and told to fill them with sand and pile them against the wall. After about an hour of this, a voice over the loudspeaker said, "That's enough. Now get those stones and pile them up near the sand bags. When the White Devils come, we need those stones to throw at them." I looked at the boys on the other side of the yard, and saw that they were doing something with the bamboo poles. "Line those bamboo spears neatly against the wall," said the voice over the loudspeaker. "Remember, when the White Devils come you each must grab one, and stab them."

That was my first day of school. When I went home, Mother did not ask me any questions. She looked at my dirty hands and my sunburnt face. I knew she saw that I didn't have my lunch box. I told her about my new Japanese name and I asked her to call me by my Korean name at home as often as she could. I started to sob. "Sookan, Sookan," she murmured as she held me tightly in her arms and rocked me gently. Her body felt very hot against mine, and I knew she was sick. "The war will be over soon and the Japanese will leave, right Mother?"

"Yes, yes, soon," she replied. "Soon it'll all be better." Exhausted from the afternoon, I rested my head on Mother's lap as I listened to her reassuring words. How glad I was to be at home for the evening.

I wished morning would never come, but it did, all too soon. I felt like announcing, "I am not going to that horrible place again this morning." But I knew if I didn't go to school, my family would be in trouble with Captain Narita and the police. She handed me two little balls of rice and millet wrapped in a damp white handkerchief to keep them moist. She forced a smile. Quietly, I took my lunch and left for school. I thought of all the other girls in my class who had to endure this with me. They had been there much longer than I had. Maybe it won't be so bad today, I kept thinking as I walked along the streets Aunt Tiger had shown me.

I headed straight to school. I didn't rub my eyes and try to see Grandfather, the big stone statue, or the chuckling Buddha. I wasn't as afraid as I had been the day before. I just felt tired and miserable. I had not gotten very far when someone came and tapped me on the shoulder. It was the little girl with whom I had tried to share my lunch. She looked around to make sure no one was listening and whispered in Korean, "I'm sorry to have made you first in line. Maybe we should measure who's taller . . . we can put these books on our heads and see." She told me that if we were not perfectly lined up in size order, the whole class would be punished. It was our responsibility. I thanked her and told her that it didn't really matter to me where I stood in line; it was all the same to me. She nodded and told me her name was Oknyul. I did not ask her Japanese name; we weren't allowed to talk to each other at school anyway. Oknyul then walked away, as we were not supposed to speak Korean in public. I followed her into the school yard and silently took my place in front of her.

It was an unusually hot and sticky June morning. The sun beat down on us, and our gray hats only made us feel hotter. I hated these hats we had to wear. They made us look like little soldiers.

After the "*Kimigayo*" and the pledge and the chant about the White Devils' inevitable defeat, we continued making weapons in the school yard. Each class worked in a different part of the yard. Over in the far corner the big boys were making spearheads, which they fastened onto the end of the long bamboo poles. The smaller boys were filling bags with sand. The older girls on the other side of the yard were using bricks to break big pieces of glass and rock into smaller pieces. My class was ordered to sharpen these small pieces of glass and rock to throw at the White Devils. Unhi and I tried to work side by side. When Narita Sensei told us how to make the pieces extra sharp, Unhi and I looked at each other, smiled, and nodded our heads in silent agreement. We bent our heads over our work and reveled in our secret. We rubbed the little pieces of glass and rock against the bricks and made them smooth and round. Then we hid them under the sharp pieces that the other girls had made. In our small way, we felt we were doing something good. We were proud of ourselves as we worked in silence under the watchful eyes of Narita Sensei.

Later that afternoon, Principal Watanabe stood before

us and, looking over at the older girls, told us, "You have all worked hard and done good work for the Japanese Empire. Our Heavenly Emperor is very proud of you. The many bundles of leg warmers, vests, and blankets you made are going to be sent to the Imperial soldiers." Then he looked at us and said, "Look around you; you have prepared enough sharp little pieces of glass and rock to hurt the White Devils if they should come here and attack us." Unhi and I looked at each other. We knew not all the pieces were sharp. Then he looked over at the big boys and said, "Now, look at our walls. Enough spears to kill them all. Let us rehearse. When the alarm rings, your teacher will tell you where to stand and then you must all grab what is in front of you and throw it over the fence."

The afternoon sun blazed down upon us. My lips were parched and my fingers throbbed with pain. The air was muggy, and there wasn't even the slightest breeze to refresh us. I wished that man would disappear and let us rest. I was tired of all these instructions. I was sick of this school. I was mad that I was born a Korean. I was angry at everyone . . . my mother, Grandfather, Aunt Tiger, my sister hiding in the convent, my father away in Manchuria, and my brothers who were off at labor camps. I was mad at the whole world. I didn't even like Mother's God.

The principal kept droning on and on about the White Devils until suddenly one of the big boys shouted, "Stop, stop, stop! Don't you know that we will stab you bastards first! We'll help the Americans destroy you all! You killers!"

The students gasped. But I clapped my hands in delight. I couldn't help myself. Listening to this boy was as refreshing as diving into a cool stream. Then I realized all the first and second grade girls standing around me were staring in silent horror. Narita Sensei came over to me and hit me so hard that I fell to my knees crying. Principal Watanabe shouted something I didn't understand and a group of teachers rushed over to the boy and took him away. Everyone was ordered to stand at attention. A group punishment would be decided on. We were all in trouble, and we all knew we would never see that poor, outspoken boy ever again.

Narita Sensei told me to follow her to Principal Watanabe's office. I was very scared and exhausted from the heat. I must have fainted. When I came to, the school yard was dark and I saw Mother looking down at me holding a wet handkerchief to my forehead. Mother said that Unhi was sent to fetch her; many other children had fainted as they were kept standing under the hot sun for so long. I felt ashamed. She and Grandfather always tried to teach me to be peaceful and merciful, but I couldn't help it. I saw all the spears against the wall, and I couldn't help thinking how wonderful it would be to kill all those wicked Japanese as that boy had said. I didn't know how to change these awful feelings. Mother didn't scold me. Instead, she whispered in my ear, "The war will be over

81

soon. You can see it. The police are acting more frantic and desperate every day." She assured me it did not matter that I had gotten expelled.

The next several days were more difficult than ever. What little rice we were once able to buy was no longer available. They wouldn't sell us rice at any price. We ate all the barley and millet we had and whatever else we could find just to stay alive. We chewed on dandelion roots to try to appease our hunger, but our stomachs ached. Finally, after four days, Captain Narita made an announcement. He said the merchants had a limited amount of rice that could be purchased in return for very precious objects. This had happened before. It was their way of stripping us of whatever else we might still be hiding. Mother sighed. "They keep us hungry, and when the babies cry for food and the grandparents are weak and sick from hunger, mothers will sacrifice even their most cherished items for a small cupful of rice."

Mother took her silver hairpin off. Her long braid fell to her waist. She looked sadly at the tarnished pin that had once belonged to her mother, and she ran her finger over the little embossed flowers and birds. She handed it to me. "Let's polish it," she said. "Maybe it will get us enough rice for dinner. Captain Narita and the Japanese merchants probably think we still have some gold left, but this little bit of silver is all I have." For the first time, I would see how beautiful it was. While I worked, Mother fixed her hair with a wooden stick she had found in Grandfather's whittling basket. Aunt Tiger, who had been watching in silence, took off a small gold pin that she was wearing hidden on her undershirt. It had been a wedding gift from her husband. Together they went and joined the long line of ladies all hoping for a small bag of rice. I was ashamed. I did not stop Mother and Aunt Tiger from going. But I knew that if it were not for Inchun and me, they would have kept those precious items and waited a little longer. As they left, I heard Mother sigh to Aunt Tiger, "Will this never end?"

They were gone for a long time. They finally came back with a tiny bag of rice. "Soon we will have something decent to eat," said Mother as she walked into the kitchen. Suddenly, we heard her gasp. We ran into the kitchen and saw that the bowl into which Mother had poured the bag of rice was half filled with sand.

"They did it again," said Aunt Tiger. "Even when they sell us so little, they mix it . . ." Aunt knelt on a clean straw mat. She had a deep fan-shaped straw container into which she put some rice and swirled it around making the grains dance. The white grains of rice flew out of the container and landed on the clean mat while the heavy sand remained in the container. Aunt was so skillful that I knew she had done this before.

That night we each had a few precious mouthfuls of white rice for dinner.

Chapter Six

August brought wild winds and torrential rains to Kirimni. The long days of summer were swelteringly humid, and the dense air weighed heavily upon us. It was more than Mother could stand. She lay in bed burning with fever. She could not retain any food. She became thinner and paler each day. Sometimes she would mumble and cry in a delirium. She talked to Grandfather as if he were sitting next to her. She often called out to the sock girls. She asked for her sons, but not for Inchun and me. When she opened her eyes and saw us sitting next to her, she didn't recognize us. She would close her eyes again and resume talking to people who were not there.

One day Inchun started to shake her. "Mother," he screamed. "Nobody is here but *Nuna* and me! Why don't you talk to us? Why can't you look at us?" He began to sob uncontrollably. I told him to stop, but crying was exactly what I felt like doing. Mother had always been the one to nurse us back to health. I was afraid. When Grandfather took to his bed, he went to join his merciful

Buddha. Maybe Mother would too. Or she would go to see her Catholic God in Heaven.

Aunt Tiger sent Kisa to the convent to see if they had any special medicine. She also wanted to know if the convent would make an exception and let Theresa come home for a few days. When Aunt asked for Theresa, I knew she was afraid Mother would die. Maybe seeing her firstborn would be enough to make Mother well again. Mother was so proud of Theresa's religious calling, and talked about her all the time. Theresa looked just like Mother, too. She was tall and very fair, with large almond eyes. Whenever Mother spoke of Theresa, I couldn't help feeling a tinge of jealousy. Once I asked her why she didn't talk of me and miss me as she missed Theresa.

"You say the craziest things!" said Mother. "You are here with me all the time. How can I miss you?" We laughed and laughed and I felt very silly. Theresa had not been home for as long as I could remember, but I often thought how wonderful it would be if she were with us. I couldn't wait until Kisa returned home; maybe he would bring the medicine and Theresa.

Kisa came through the gate walking quickly, tipping from side to side. I thought he might fall over. He was back earlier than we had expected. He waved his arms in excitement all the while as he tried to catch his breath. "The war is over!" he blurted out. "The war is over! Japan has lost! The nuns got a message from the Bishop, who heard the Emperor surrender unconditionally. But the Bishop told the nuns to be very careful and to stay indoors, because it is more dangerous than ever to anger the Japanese now. Most Koreans don't know yet, and the Japanese aren't anxious to spread the news. They want to retreat safely first. For now, they have all the weapons and are still in power here. We have to be careful." Kisa pulled out a small package and handed it to Aunt, saying, "Reverend Mother said that the nuns shouldn't be traveling now, but she thinks this medicine will help. You all stay inside for now. I'll be back." He swung his arms back and forth vigorously to help propel himself to town.

It was August 15, 1945, a day I would always remember as if it were my own birthday. I ran to Mother's room and cried, "Mother, the war is over! You have to get up, you have to get up!" I shook her.

Aunt Tiger came and pulled me away. "She is getting a little bit better, but you must give her time," she whispered urgently. "Come with me. Let's prepare some of this medicine for her." I did everything Aunt Tiger said. I didn't want Mother to leave me. The day she had been praying for had finally arrived. Inchun and I stayed beside her the rest of the afternoon and fed her the medicine that Kisa brought from the convent.

Late in the afternoon, Kisa came hopping back on his good leg. He didn't have the patience to limp. As he drew near the house, he shouted, "We're free! We're free! I've been telling everyone. The flag with the bloodshot sun is being taken down. They are putting up *our* flag!" Then, he fell to the floor as if his left leg could not support all the excitement within him. He started to weep. Aunt Tiger fell to her knees beside him and hugged him. Crying with joy and relief, they ran out into the yard, fell to their knees, and kissed the ground. Inchun and I stared at them. Tears filled my eyes.

I kept hoping that Mother would get up and rejoice with them. Inchun and I watched her sleeping. Then we shook her and screamed, "You have to wake up! Look, Mother, look! Kisa and Aunt Tiger are going crazy."

To our delight, she opened her eyes and weakly murmured, "What is happening?"

"Mother, the war is over!" we shouted. "The war is over just as you always said! Kisa found out when he went to the convent."

Mother closed her eyes and whispered, "I knew my God would not forsake me." Her lips quivered and tears streamed down her pale, sunken cheeks. "Your father will return soon . . . and your brothers and the sock girls. If they are alive, they will all be home soon." Inchun and I held her trembling hands and listened to her mumble for a long time before she finally fell back asleep. We watched her begin to breathe evenly and then tiptoed outside to see Kisa and Aunt Tiger.

Aunt Tiger was busy talking about all the things she would do when her husband returned from the Japanese labor camp, and I knew that Kisa was thinking of the sock girls. Aunt Tiger said that all the Koreans who had been imprisoned by the Japanese police would be released. For now, there was little we could do but wait for the Japanese to leave. I hoped my father and brothers would return soon, and I wished that Theresa would come home. I resented all of them for being away, especially now when Mother was so sick.

Kisa told Inchun and me not to go outside. It was dangerous, for the streets were filled with Japanese residents guarded by the Japanese police as they retreated from Korea. Kisa told us that some of the Koreans were so overjoyed to be free of the Japanese that they were smashing the Shinto shrines and defiling the temples. But they had been too impetuous. The Japanese soldiers and police were still everywhere with their swords and guns. They did not hesitate to kill the Koreans. Some of the frustrated townspeople then began attacking the pro-Japanese Koreans who had lived in relative comfort all these years. Aunt Tiger and Kisa were dismayed by such violence. It was a time to rejoice in our newfound freedom and peace and to begin planning our new lives.

Inchun and I stayed indoors with Mother for the next few days while Aunt Tiger and Kisa went about keeping abreast of the latest happenings. Inchun and I stayed by Mother's side, bringing her cool compresses and giving her the medicine that Kisa had brought from the convent. Her fever finally broke. She was able to retain some food and regained some color in her cheeks. She rested in bed quietly. After a couple of days, she got up and walked around the house. With Mother up and about, Inchun and I felt at last we could truly rejoice. I suddenly wanted to do all the things that I had been dreaming of for all these years.

With Kisa's help, Inchun and I staked out a small plot in the front yard, and put some rope up around it. Then, Inchun and I dug furrows in the barren earth. I ran to get the packages of seeds. The paper was so old it crumbled to bits as I opened the packages. We planted all the seeds we had, not knowing what was in season. We just planted everything. I asked Mother to find some azalea seeds. I wanted to see flowers of all colors surround me. Mother laughed. "Not everything grows from seeds, you know." She was still weak, but she sat and watched as we ran about in the dirt. "Leave a little path for us to walk so we can garden," she murmured happily. I couldn't wait for the marigolds, dandelions, wild lilies, and pansies to burst into bloom. It was so wonderful to be free! No more Japanese school, no more speaking Japanese, no more Naritas, no more fear, no more, no more!

Mother asked Kisa and Aunt Tiger to get out the big brown earthen *kimchee*-jar hidden in the kitchen. Inchun and I offered to help, but Mother said, "No, from now on, no more grown-up chores and worries for my children. You are going to play, and read and enjoy the carefree days of childhood. Leave everything to the grown-ups." Aunt Tiger and Kisa smiled and pushed us away.

I grabbed Inchun and we ran into Grandfather's room. I yanked off the drab tablecloth that hid Grandfather's beautiful hand-carved scholar's desk. How wonderful it was to be able to enjoy this beautiful desk and know that no one would take it from us anymore. I opened all the drawers and took out the oxtail brushes, the black slate inkwell, and Grandfather's Chinese books. I spread them out on the table and said, "There, Inchun, you can sit and draw all you want and copy all those letters and drawings all day long. You no longer have to draw in the dirt with wooden twigs."

"But I like drawing in the dirt," he said.

"Well, now you can do whatever you want." Inchun plopped himself down in front of the scholar's desk and with a flourish picked up a brush.

I ran to Mother's room, took out the record player that the nuns had given me, and dragged out all four of my records: the Brahms lullabies, Beethoven's Ninth Symphony, Mozart sonatas, and a collection of American songs with "Oh My Darling Clementine" and "Home on the Range." I spread them out on the floor for everybody to see. I cranked up the old record player and put Beethoven on with the volume way up. No more hiding under blankets late at night with the volume so low we had to strain our ears to listen. The sun was shining brightly and I jumped around humming and combing my hair. I shouted to Inchun, who was in the next room, "Do you hear that, Inchun? Come here and listen to the music!" "The whole town can hear it," said Mother. "We are free, but not free of manners. Turn it down, don't make us all go deaf!" Through her scolding, I detected the twinkle in her eyes.

Later, Mother called us out to the yard for a surprise. The Japanese flag that had flown in front of the entrance to our house for as long as I could remember was now replaced by our Korean flag. How strange it was to see our beautiful flag so boldly displayed. Then she led us into my room. On the floor, she had laid out several beautiful silk *hanbok* — Korean outfits — in bright red, green, pink, white, and blue. The red one had a beautiful rainbow pattern on the sleeves and at the bottom of the skirt, and the pale blue one had silver trim and deep blue flowers embroidered on it. I chose the pale blue *hanbok* with the flowers on it and rubbed it against my cheek. It smelled musty from being buried in the earthen jar for so long. I ran into the other room, pulled off my drab gray outfit, and put on the elegant dress. I felt so grand.

Kisa put on a crisp white outfit which must have belonged to Grandfather. Mother put on the white *hanbok*, and Aunt Tiger the green one. Mother had given Inchun a pair of American shorts and a button-down shirt. His little bony knees stuck out awkwardly. He looked down at his legs and asked, "Can I put my old pants back on?"

"Whatever pleases you," replied Mother. How strange. I had never heard that before. How wonderful it was to be free. We listened to our records, drew pictures, and read. We tended our garden, watering it several times a day, and lifting the seedlings out of the ground to look at the roots. Beside the garden we set up a playhouse made from Grandfather's canes and one of Mother's sheets.

As the days passed, the grown-ups became increasingly anxious. Mother waited expectantly for Father and my three brothers, and Aunt Tiger went out several times a day to see if anyone had any news about her husband. Kisa waited anxiously for any news of the sock girls. Cries of joy and sorrow filled the streets. Men began returning from the front and from the jails, but they too often brought with them news of those who had died.

One day, Aunt Tiger came back from one of her excursions and said, "I hear most of the Japanese soldiers and the police have left. It's safe for us to go anywhere we want now, I think. I want to go see the Naritas' house. I spent so many years cleaning that house. Now I'd like to take a walk there and enjoy myself." I wanted to go with her, and started to follow. Mother was concerned, but Aunt Tiger assured her that many Koreans had already moved back into their former homes that the Japanese had taken from them, and that it would be safe for me to come along.

Aunt Tiger took my hand, and we walked through the streets in our colorful silk *hanbok*, speaking freely in Korean. Many Koreans were out in their *hanbok*, talking, laughing, and crying. Korean flags were proudly flying in front of almost every home. Gone were the gray uniforms and the masses of silent people walking with their heads lowered in subservience and fear. How wonderful it was to know that no police would come and frighten us off. We walked through the bustling streets of Kirimni and turned toward the hills.

Aunt Tiger pointed to the houses that dotted the hills and said, "The rightful Korean owners should be coming back to all these homes now. This is where all the Japanese government officials and rich merchants lived." Up a smooth gravel-covered path, we finally came upon a beautiful house of greenish-gray brick with a big wooden gate that stood ajar. "This house used to be occupied by the Naritas," Aunt Tiger said.

I looked at this beautiful house where the Naritas had lived and asked Aunt, "Can we go in and see the inside?"

"I suppose we can if no one's living here already," Aunt Tiger said. "I'll give you the tour."

We walked into the yard and suddenly the sliding door to one of the rooms opened. To my great surprise, Unhi was staring straight at me. "Well, don't just stand there. If you came to see me, come inside quickly." She spoke abruptly, just as she had on my first day of school. Aunt and I looked at each other in disbelief and stepped inside.

"I was thinking of you," said Unhi. "I was going to look for you. How do you like our house? This house used to belong to my grandfather. Some Japanese government officials threw him in jail because he refused to give up his house. And after that, my grandmother and aunts still refused to move out. So then, some Japanese soldiers came, and started to undress them and tried to attack them. My grandmother and aunts went running. They were lucky they got away."

"Unhi!" shouted her mother, who was coming out to greet us. "My Unhi talks too much. Please come and sit.

They took all the furniture and all our things with them, but we're back in the family house."

Aunt Tiger and Unhi's mother sat by the little fishpond in the yard. Unhi and I talked in Korean about all the things we had always wanted to tell each other at school. Hours went by. Suddenly I remembered Mother would be waiting for us. I was so excited to see Unhi that I had completely forgotten. I went and got Aunt Tiger, and we rushed home. Just as we had imagined, Mother was standing by the gate, looking down the road. She scolded us, but was happy to hear about our visit with Unhi and her mother. I went to sleep that night thinking of the many nice surprises in store for me.

The next morning, as Inchun and I were watering the garden, the gate swung open. In walked Unhi and her mother. I had told Unhi where we lived, but she hadn't said anything about coming by. Her mother asked to see my mother. While they visited, I showed Unhi my garden. Inchun followed us everywhere. Unhi kept staring at him. "Is he mute?" she finally asked. "How come he never says anything? What a strange one!"

Inchun just grinned, and I ruffled his hair. If Unhi only knew how clever and wise he was. Unhi looked at us and said, "Yeah, well, like I said that first day I saw you, you're a funny one, too." Then Unhi told us that after we left the night before, she and her mother went to check the secret storage compartment in the basement and found it full of sacks of rice. They came to us today to ask for our help in distributing the rice to the rest of the townspeople.

Kisa worked all day distributing the sacks of white rice. Mother and Aunt Tiger could not take their eyes off our bag. "It must be a good ten pounds," said Mother. "I haven't seen that much rice in my home since the Japanese arrived. We'll have to make a special dinner tonight."

"We must divide the rice into smaller bags and put them in a cool dry place," added Aunt Tiger. "That way, the bugs and mice won't get at it."

As Aunt Tiger rushed around to find small bags to store it in, Mother smiled to herself and whispered to me, "Your Aunt is pretending that we are back in the old days when we had a roomful of rice to keep for the entire season. This sack won't be around long enough to go bad or get eaten by mice." But she just watched Aunt play with the dainty grains of white rice, putting them into small bags and tying them carefully.

Aunt Tiger learned from a neighbor that two of Unhi's brothers had come back from a Japanese labor camp and were very ill. Unhi's mother came to talk to Mother a few days later and told how her boys had been forced to dig ditches sixteen hours a day under the hot sun and the pouring rain. They survived on potato roots and some mixed grains. The Japanese soldiers often amused themselves by forcing the boys to drink their own urine. She cried as she recounted these terrible stories.

The dreams of a happy future together in a free land were shattered. The whole town was transformed into a hospital. Many men and boys came home only to die. There were many funeral processions every day, and wailing and sobbing filled the air. It was as if all the sadness and misery that had to go unexpressed for the past thirty-six years had been unleashed. "I don't know which is better, not to see my boys and cling to the hope that they are alive and healthy, or to have them come home so sick that I have to watch them die," said Mother to Aunt Tiger.

The next day, we heard that both of Unhi's brothers had died. I saw Unhi's mother in the funeral procession, dressed in the traditional burlap funeral gown, and behind her, I saw Unhi. Unhi's mother was wailing, and pounding her chest as if she wanted to die and join her sons. But I couldn't take my eyes off Unhi as she walked behind the two coffins and rubbed the tears from her eyes. That dull burlap funeral outfit made her look like a dying old woman. I felt like a million years had gone by since that day when we had talked so happily at her big house. How quickly our world kept changing.

Kisa kept checking the train station hoping to see the sock girls, my brothers, Father, and Aunt Tiger's husband. One day he came running home and said, "We'd better lock the door. The Russians are in the next town over. For the past few days, they've been picking up all the young men who are reasonably healthy and are taking them to Siberia. Many Russian soldiers have been looting houses and attacking the village people, especially the women. They have special guns that can fire many shots in quick succession and can kill many people all at once."

Mother and Aunt Tiger were not as shocked as I was. It seemed they knew something about it. I thought the Americans would be coming back to see us, but I had never thought about the Russians. I didn't know much about the Russians, but Grandfather had told me he didn't trust them. He said the Russians always wanted to own Korea just as the Japanese and the Chinese had. "Korea was a little shrimp caught in a struggle between giants," he had said.

Mother and Aunt Tiger took off their bright *hanbok* and put on their gray workers' outfits. At Kisa's insistence, Mother and Aunt tied scarves over their heads and smeared dirt and ash on their cheeks to make themselves look older than they were. Reluctantly, I took off my colorful *hanbok* and put on my old gray outfit. We stayed inside the house with the doors locked and thick blankets hanging from the rice-paper paneled doors to make the house appear dark and deserted.

"Where are the Americans? Why are the Russians here now?" Aunt sighed.

"The Russians live closer to us, they are practically our next-door neighbors," replied Mother. "It will take a while for the Americans to get here, but they will be here. They won't let the Russians stay. The Russians are probably here to make sure the Japanese leave safely."

"Who is going to hurt the Japanese?" Aunt Tiger

retorted. "They have their guns and soldiers and we have none." Mother said nothing. We spent several days hiding in our dark house. At night, we sometimes heard pots and pans rattling. Aunt Tiger told me it was a signal to warn everyone that the Russian soldiers were around. Mother and Aunt Tiger had seen the Russian soldiers in the streets when they ventured outside during the day. But I had not yet seen any of them because I had stayed inside all the time.

Later we learned that the Russian soldiers had been in Korea for quite a while, some said since early August, before the Emperor officially surrendered. They had come to drive out the Japanese. Some of our neighbors said they liked the Russians for chasing out the Japanese, and hailed them as liberators. Many Koreans, who had been waiting for the Americans, were hurt and disappointed. "At least the Russians care enough to come," they said. "We should be good to them." Others feared that the Russians would soon treat us just as the Japanese had. Mother said the Russians would soon leave, but others said that they were here to stay. They said that Korea had been divided into two at the 38th parallel. The Russians were in the northern part for good.

I was curious about these Russians, and when I saw their trucks rumble by, I wished I could get a closer look at them. I heard that many Russian soldiers had no hair at all because they had come straight from jail. Some called them green-eyed barbarians. They ate everything in sight, chased girls, and stole whatever they could carry. They ate in the streets as they walked, kicking passersby with their big feet. They carried huge guns with round disks.

We still had no news of my father, my brothers, or the sock girls. We didn't know what to think. They could be anywhere. They might not even be alive. Hiding in our dark house, trapped with our fears and worries, had become oppressive. Did the Americans know how long we had been waiting for them? Did they know how Grandfather and Mother were counting on them, or how Unhi and I had rounded the edges of the little pieces of glass and rock at the Japanese school so that they would not be hurt? I decided to hum and try to forget.

While I was humming "Swannee River," Inchun got up and peered out the rice-paper paneled door. He beckoned to me. There were two Russians in our yard! One was young and tall, and had the most beautiful blue eyes, and a head of wavy yellow hair. He wore a big khaki wool coat and high boots. At his side was a huge gun. This gun was not long and thin like those of the Japanese; instead it had a huge round barrel. The other soldier had the same type of gun slung over his shoulder. He was a bit shorter and much older, and had no hair at all. Each of them had a long loaf of dark bread tucked under his left arm and each had a little pouch hanging from his neck. The older soldier reached into the pouch, took out a handful of sunflower seeds, and threw them into his mouth. Then he tore off a big bite of bread and chewed vigorously. All of a sudden, a trail of sunflower seed shells came shooting from his mouth. The younger soldier started eating, too. The two of them left a carpet of shells as they walked around the yard.

The Russians peeked into the sock factory and seemed rather disappointed to find it empty. Then they headed toward the house. As we saw them approach, we retreated to the far corner of the room. We didn't know what they would do to us. I felt stupid for having stood there watching them when we should have been trying to hide. They pushed the door open with their guns, ripped the rice-paper paneled doors, and stepped inside. I stood in front of Inchun, wedging him into the corner of the room. I was his *nuna*. I had to protect him. The men looked around and were surprised to see us. We stood in the corner gripped with fear.

As the young soldier walked past us, he chewed busily, and spewed a trail of sunflower seed shells onto our clean *ondol* floor. He spit them out in such quick succession that they seemed to form a rainbow. They both ate so ravenously that I thought if they gave us a hard time, I could offer them some of the rice cakes that Aunt Tiger had made. They poked around the house, touching and examining everything — our books and records, Mother's Bible, our clothes. Seeing the alarm clock that Aunt Tiger managed to get her hands on after the Japanese had left, the older soldier put it to his ear, listened to it tick, and happily put it in his coat pocket.

In Mother's chest, they found Father's wristwatch that Mother had managed to hide for so long. The young one picked it up. He lifted his left coat sleeve. Watches covered his entire forearm, so he checked his other arm, already adorned with several watches. He added Father's to his collection. We stood there and watched in silence. Alarm clocks and trinkets hung from their thick leather belts, which clanked and jingled as they walked. We could see brightly colored Korean silk draped around their necks. They looked proud of their collection.

Having taken everything they deemed valuable, they came over to us. The young one with the beautiful blue eyes and pretty hair said, "*Khorosho*" with a smile. Inchun held on to me tightly. The young soldier peered over at Inchun and smiled. He pointed to his bald companion and said, "Comrade." Then, he said "*Khorosho*" again. It seemed to me that he was saying "hello," but later I learned that he was trying to tell us, "It's all right." Inchun repeated after him. The young soldier lifted Inchun up, twirled him in midair, and laughed. I screamed. I was afraid they would hurt him. I held my arms out for my little brother and the soldier put him down gently and patted Inchun's soft black hair. Looking at us tenderly, he bent down and pointed to himself. "Ivan Malenkiv," he said.

We both stood there in silence and stared at him. I didn't want him to touch Inchun again. They had taken what they wanted, and spat seeds all over our clean house. I wanted them to leave. But they were not cruel like the Japanese, and even though they carried those huge guns, I wasn't as terrified of them as I had been of

Captain Narita. I wondered why. Maybe it was because their blue eyes and yellow hair reminded me of Father Carroll. As Ivan Malenkiv smiled at us so warmly, I thought that maybe we could become friends sometime. He patted us on the head, motioned to his companion, and they climbed out through the torn rice-paper paneled door.

Chapter Seven

The Russian soldiers roamed the streets of Kirimni and the smell of dark bread permeated the air. I stood by the gate watching with fascination as they meandered about, laughing and talking loudly in Russian while eating and drinking. Although it was only late September, they wore heavy wool coats, long black boots, and thick fur hats. Some took their hats off, revealing their hairless pink scalps. Mother told me to come inside, for she, like many of the other townspeople, was afraid of these "giant barbarians with their special guns." Inchun obeyed Mother, but I was too curious.

As I stood by the gate, I felt as though I had been transported to a distant land. The cruel and oppressive memories of the Japanese were still fresh, yet the whole town had been transformed, filled with sounds and smells that were so different. "*Khorosho, khorosho,* Comrade," the Russian soldiers yelled repeatedly.

A jeep drove by slowly, and a familiar voice called out in Korean from a loudspeaker, "Hello, Comrade!" It was our neighbor Mrs. Kim, riding in the jeep beside a tall, pretty, blue-eyed woman with yellow hair.

Mrs. Kim called out in Korean, "Comrades, Comrades! We are all comrades and are all equal in the eyes of Mother Russia. No one will ever again have to worry about being cold or hungry. We will share the fruits of our labors. Our Russian comrades and our party leaders are here to protect us. They are our friends. Come to the town square. See how our Korean flag flies proudly alongside the Russian flag! We are friends and partners. The capitalistic Americans have not come here because they know how poor we are now that the Japanese have extracted all the gold, tungsten, and coal from our mines. But the Russians have come to help us start anew. Come to the square and celebrate. There is food and drink for all comrades, young and old, men and women alike."

It was the first time I had ever heard Korean being spoken so loudly in the street. I shook my head to be sure I wasn't dreaming. Only a few weeks before, I had been hit for whispering in Korean. My neighbors started to come out of their homes and were staring at the jeep incredulously. Mother, Aunt Tiger, and Inchun came out, too, and stood right behind me in amazement. I began to follow the jeep with the others, but Mother grabbed me by the arm. "You are not going anywhere," she told me. "We are waiting right here until your father and brothers come. Then we are going south to where the Americans are." I wanted to follow the crowd and see what was happening, but she tightened her grip. I was furious.

"What are you talking about? What's happening?" Aunt Tiger whispered to Mother. "You don't think the Americans are coming?"

"I sent Kisa to the convent this morning. He found out that the Americans are staying in the south. They've split our country in two and established a border called the Thirty-eighth Parallel. Many Koreans have begun to flee to the South. But it's become very dangerous. The Russians shoot at anyone who attempts to cross the border. It's too soon to tell what will happen. We must wait and see. Meanwhile we must be prepared." Then Mother looked sternly at me. I knew what that meant. Everything we talked about here was secret and I must never repeat anything. Inchun also looked at me sternly, and I had to laugh.

Days went by. Many of our neighbors who had gone to the town square had joined the Russians. Mrs. Kim gave them three books written in our own *Hangul.* One of the old ladies next door who didn't know how to read came to Mother in tears. "Please, will you read these books to me?" she begged. "I haven't see a book written in Korean since the Japanese took my husband away." She started to sob.

To soothe her, Mother offered her tea and sweet rice cakes. "I am sure Comrade Kim will read them to you," she said. "For now, come and join us." She put her arm around our neighbor and led her inside. The lady showed us a red book with her Korean name written in *Hangul.* After she had gone, Mother sighed. "The Russians are so clever," she told us. "We have been starved and treated like slaves for so long that we can be won over with a few kind gestures. People don't realize they're being brainwashed."

"Can you blame them?" snapped Aunt. "How are they to know there's anything better? Your Americans aren't here. I heard they're in Japan helping the Japanese! They're nearby now, but they just don't care about us!"

The next day, Comrade Kim came to visit. She was accompanied by the pretty blue-eyed woman with yellow hair. I was so happy that I ran toward them. I was drawn to the woman's pretty eyes and the red badges on her uniform. Comrade Kim smiled at me. "This is Comrade Natasha," she said, patting me on the head. "Comrade," she added, "this is our smart little comrade Sookan. She can attend the Little Proletariat School."

"*Mulnon*," Natasha replied, which means "of course" in Korean. It was strangely exhilarating to hear this woman with the blue eyes and yellow hair speak Korean. But before I could respond, Mother came out and grabbed me by the arm. Then she smiled and greeted Mrs. Kim and Natasha. When Mrs. Kim asked where Aunt Tiger was, Mother seized the opportunity to send me inside to get her. Natasha smiled as she saw Aunt Tiger approaching and said, "*Anyong haseyo*," meaning "How are you?" Aunt Tiger was taken aback to hear Natasha greet her in Korean. All she could do was nod in response.

With the grown-ups of the household assembled,

Natasha gave us three books and asked us to come to the town meeting that evening. It was more of an order than an invitation. Comrade Kim commented that we were one of the few families that had not yet joined. Smiling, she said, "It is best to join to ensure the safety of our men. The Russian officers want a description of your husbands and sons. They will help search for them and make sure they come home to us." Having said that, she knew Mother would not refuse to come.

That evening, a jeep with a loudspeaker drove by to lead us up the hill to the meeting. We went out into the street and joined the happy masses. It was fun to be part of such a high-spirited and boisterous crowd, laughing and shouting in Korean. We walked along the path that ran along the base of the hill of Unhi's house. I looked up at the house and barely recognized it. A huge Korean flag and a huge Russian flag flew side by side, and giant portraits of Stalin and Lenin had been hung from the building. An old man gazed up the hill saying, "Under the Japanese, we were not even good enough to walk in this part of town where they all lived. Now our flag has been raised along with the Russians'." Mother and Aunt just walked on in silence.

When we arrived, Comrade Kim greeted us with a big smile and handed us each a red book with our names on it. "This is your I.D. card," she told us. "You should bring it with you to your nightly meetings." Another woman handed us red arm bands. Natasha gave us red scarves to wear around our heads. The large room was already filled with people. When everyone had arrived, Natasha started singing a spirited tune about the Volga River and Mother Russia. The crowds quickly learned the refrain and began to sing the praises of Communism.

Then she sang a catchy tune that I liked: "We the little proletariat of Mother Russia are secret leaders. Small but important comrades, important leaders. Bad Capitalists, bad Imperialists. Marxism is the best. Our leaders, our leaders, they are our friends. We share equally. We are all friends, we are all equals. Little proletariat can do important work. We are important, we are important, we are important comrades." I sang out loud and was happy until I looked over at Mother and Aunt. I realized that they were barely mouthing the words. I felt guilty for enjoying myself so much, but everyone else, even Inchun, seemed to be having a good time at this festive gathering.

After a few more songs, we ate a huge meal and then were told to sit in front of a big screen. We were to watch a film about Mother Russia. I had wondered what Russia was like, and I couldn't wait for the movie to begin. The lights dimmed, and loud Russian music started to play. Masses of happy Russian proletarians filled the screen, waving red flags as they marched and danced in Red Square in celebration of May Day. Then I saw the vast fields of golden wheat and the happy farmers. The narrator said, "Mother Russia is a workers' paradise. No one wants for anything in wonderful Mother Russia."

We came home very late and I was exhausted. Mother

and Aunt said nothing on the way back. Early the next morning, at the crack of dawn, we were awakened by a loudspeaker. "Comrades, rise and shine. The sun is up. The happy proletariat of Mother Russia must begin to build the workers' paradise. There are streets to be swept, fields to be cleared, and crops to be planted. Here are your hoes, rakes, and brooms. Come." We donned our red scarves and red arm bands and went outside. One of the Russian comrades was standing at our gate waiting, and counted to see that we were all there. He put us on a truck which stopped at house after house until the vehicle was full.

We were driven to the outskirts of the city. One Russian comrade rode in the back with us and led us in song as we sped along. Mother and Aunt along with several other women were dropped off near an old minefield. They were to clear the land. Inchun and I and several other children were dropped off at a factory to sweep and clean. Inchun and I swept the grounds for several hours. At lunchtime, we were driven to another large building already filled with people. We looked for Mother and Aunt, but couldn't find them. So, Inchun and I ate with the other children. Soon we were taken back to the work site. Late in the afternoon, they picked us up and said we were going to see a movie. We drank barley tea, and sat down in front of the large screen. It was the same movie we had seen the night before. I was glad when it ended and the truck took us back home. Mother and Aunt were getting off another truck as we pulled in, and we ran to their waiting arms. Exhausted from the hard work, Inchun and I tumbled into bed.

Every day was more or less the same. We worked, sang variations of the same old songs, heard the same praises of Communism and Mother Russia, and saw the same happy faces of the Russian proletariat in the movie they showed over and over again. Incessantly, the loudspeaker blared the praises of the great Russian leaders. The town was so noisy I could hardly think. There was no need to think. Our every activity from dawn to dusk was programmed for us. We wore identical black pants, white shirts, and red scarves, and each morning when we were picked up for work, we were told what to do and how to do it. I had not learned anything new since that first Party meeting. I had begun to realize that Mother and Aunt were right.

Every day the Russians criticized the capitalistic Americans to make us feel the way they did. I found it harder and harder to tolerate the Korean women who worked so hard for the Party, fervently spreading Communist philosophy. They were so happy and proud to be leaders, and we called them our Town Reds. I was tired of it all, but there was no choice. We had to go to work and to the Party meetings every day to have our red I.D. books stamped. Each week, they counted the stamps before they gave us our rice ration.

The monotonous days turned into weeks and then months. It had been almost a year, and my father and brothers had still not returned. Aunt Tiger continued to wait for her husband. I missed the sock girls and I wished we could see even one of them. But we had no news of them. Our town was sparkling clean, and the red Russian flags, the red banners, and the big pictures of the "kind Marxist leaders" were everywhere.

Everything seemed to be in perfect order, but once in a while, we would hear of people trying to escape to the South. The dedicated Town Reds started a campaign to identify traitors. Over the loudspeaker they made their announcements: "Comrades, beware of the traitors who try to escape to the capitalistic South. Russia has no mercy for traitors. Those who have tried have been shot to death." Every time we heard these announcements, we couldn't help worrying whether we were on "the list." As Aunt Tiger put it, we weren't like the Town Reds, we were "Phony Reds" or "Pinks" who reluctantly did as we were told.

The special school for "The Little Proletariat" was finally established. Instead of attending the Party meetings with the grown-ups, we had our own meetings. With Natasha and Comrade Kim, we sang special songs and while we ate, we watched that same old movie. We were constantly told how important we were. Comrade Kim said it was our duty as little proletarians to teach the grown-ups. If we knew of grown-ups who did not show complete dedication to the Party, we should come and tell Comrade Kim and Natasha, and they would help us. They encouraged us to talk about our families and tell them what we talked about at night. Many of the children told stories about what their families were doing and received prizes for their candor. Inchun and I said as little as possible. We were not very popular at the Little Proletariat School. A little boy named Hansin was so thrilled to be a little proletarian that he talked all the time. One day he mentioned that a stranger had come to his house, and after that we never saw him or his family again. I started to grow more and more afraid of the Russians and the Town Reds.

Mother worried about our going to the Little Proletariat School. I heard her say to Aunt Tiger, "After all, they are children and the Town Reds are very skillful at getting information out of them." She was right. With each passing day, it got more difficult for Inchun and me to say so little.

We knew that Kisa was trying to make some arrangements for us all to go South. Mother wanted us to be ready to leave as soon as Father, my brothers, and the nuns arrived. As a mechanic, Kisa was always going around fixing things, and he got to know many of the Pinks in town. He became involved with a group that helped locate secret guides that would take people to the South. As a cover, he pretended to be a Town Red, actively working for the Party. Mother said he would be killed if they found out what he was doing. At home, Inchun and I would sit together and make up things to tell the comrades. We kept working and attending the school, but it was all very boring. I began to wonder what it would be like in the South.

The cold weather was setting in. Mrs. Kim brought a barrel full of coal for us to warm our shiny *ondol* floor. Beaming, she told us, "Your Kisa works so hard for the Party. He often works all through the night to recruit Party members. So we have brought your family the first batch of coal to help keep you warm. Remember how freezing cold we always were when the Japanese Imperialists were here?" Mother nodded and thanked her.

Early the next morning, Kisa came rushing home and whispered to Mother, "We'll have to make plans to go to the South right away. It's getting tougher and tougher. The Russians have discovered most of the secret paths we've been using, and they've started closing them off. They've put more guards on patrol with machine guns. We think a lot of the people we sent have been killed, but we're not sure."

"I want to wait as long as we can for the nuns and for the men so that we can all go together," said Mother.

Kisa shook his head. "They're probably already in the South," he said. "Many men went straight to the South when they were released by the Japanese. They got word of the Thirty-eighth Parallel before we did. We can't wait. If we wait much longer, we'll never be able to leave. I'm going to make the arrangements. We have to be careful to avoid suspicion. There are lots of spies around. Make sure to go to all the meetings, and smile and sing loudly."

He patted Inchun and me on the head and said, "I know I don't have to worry about you two little ones. You're too smart for your age. Keep an eye on your Mother and especially on your Aunt Tiger. Make sure she doesn't complain about anything. We all have to look like happy members of the proletariat, understood? I'll be back as soon as I can." Kisa left as quickly as he had come. We all watched him limp away.

The following morning, the truck came by and picked us up as usual. The day never seemed so long. Inchun and I worked side by side in the fields. Whenever one of the Town Reds came near us, my heart started to race and I was afraid she would shout, "Traitors, we know you are plotting to escape. You are only pretending to be good little proletarians." I was glad when the sun set and we were finally put on the truck and dropped off at home. My voice was hoarse and my arms ached because I had sung so loudly and waved the flag with the hammer and sickle so vigorously the whole way home.

The days dragged on slowly, now that I was anxiously waiting for Kisa to tell us when we would be going to the South. It was hard not knowing what had happened to my father and brothers. It was hard to remain silent when it was all that I thought about. Mrs. Kim started to bring delicious cookies to the Little Proletariat meetings to give to the children who told all about their families, but Inchun and I were wary. Our whole household was nervous and frightened. We were afraid of the Russians, but even more afraid of the converted Korean Communists, for they would surely report us. It was hard to tell who was a Pink. We couldn't take any chances.

One afternoon, Mrs. Kim came to visit us. She asked if Mother was feeling all right and if we had enough to eat. Mother thanked her profusely for her concern, and Comrade Kim left saying, "Mother Russia and our leaders are generous. If you need more bread to eat, we will give you more."

Mother sighed with relief as she watched Mrs. Kim walk back out the gate, but Aunt Tiger whispered, "Do you think she knows something? Maybe someone told her to watch us closely. I wonder if Kisa is all right . . . it's been a few days since he's been home."

"I am sure he's all right," replied Mother, wringing her hands. "Mrs. Kim is just poking about as usual."

That night we ate our meal in silence. I heard Mother and Aunt Tiger whispering their prayers in the next room. I, too, said my prayers under my breath and I drifted off to sleep, comforted by their voices.

Chapter Eight

A cold gray fog hung over the town. The rice-paper paneled doors, rattling in the late-October winds, sounded like crickets on a dark night. It was late, but we were trying to stay awake, hoping this would be the night that Kisa would come to see us. When I went to adjust the rice-paper panels, I saw a black figure limping toward us. My heart started to race and I was filled with joy and relief.

Kisa smiled nervously as he came inside. He was flushed and breathing heavily. "I saw Uncle!" he blurted out. "Just for a few minutes on the road."

Mother said, "When, how is — "

Kisa waved his arms in the air to stop her and said that he had only a few minutes to spare. He said that through his work with the Party members, he had gotten in touch with Father, who had been trying for a long time to find a way to reach us. Father had successfully convinced the Communists to hire him to transport raw materials from the North and trade them for rice in the South. He had already made several trips back and forth.

While transporting goods to the South, he managed

to help many people escape. Somehow, he found my three brothers after the war. Jaechun had been very sick with tuberculosis and dysentery due to the bad food and the years of hard labor under the Japanese. Hanchun and Hyunchun were about to be shipped off to Siberia, but Father got to them in time. Mother had her hands clasped over her mouth to contain herself. She wanted to hear every word. "Are they all right, where are they now?" she finally blurted out.

"Yes, yes, Uncle said they are all fine now," Kisa answered. "They were ill, but Uncle hid them in a Buddhist temple far in the north where they could recuperate. Then, he hid them in his truck and took them to Seoul. Uncle is looking well. He's working on coming up to Kirimni to take us back next. From now on, we must be ready to leave at a moment's notice."

"We'll be ready," Mother said. "We'll pack everything right away and we'll be waiting."

"No, no . . . no packing. There's not enough room in the truck," said Kisa. "Just be dressed in many layers of warm dark clothing. We must pretend we are off to a Party meeting down the street. We're going to have to walk through town to meet him. He can't be seen straying from his appointed route. It would arouse a lot of suspicion. In the meantime, be very visible at the Party meeting, praise Communism, and hoist the red flags high. If you can, try to be home as much as possible. I don't know when Uncle will be coming, but we have to be ready to go whenever he shows up."

"Be careful," whispered Mother, and she watched him disappear into the darkness. She stared at the door through which Kisa had so quickly come and gone, and then collapsed to the ground. I saw tears welling up in her eyes. Aunt Tiger sat next to her and they hugged each other. Mother stretched out her arms and Inchun and I ran to them. How good it was to know that Father was alive and well, and that my three brothers were safe in Seoul. And how wonderful to know that Father would be coming to take us to the South. Yet I wondered how it was that he had left us here so long. I wished that he had come for us earlier, as he had for his sons. Why had he left us for last?

Mother, wiping her tears with her trembling fingers, murmured, "I knew my God would not desert me. I knew He was listening to all our prayers." Then Mother looked at Aunt Tiger and said, "We will soon hear good news about your husband, too." I suddenly realized how pensive Aunt Tiger looked. She was happy for us, but I knew that every day she hoped for some news of her husband.

We waited in anxious excitement, and each day seemed longer than the one before. Aunt Tiger, frightened that our plan would be discovered, said one day, "I think I should be more visible at Party meetings. It'll make it easier for us. Maybe I'll be able to get us a work assignment to do at home."

Mother exclaimed, "How long do you think you can fool the eager Reds? We're all doing enough. Don't get in any deeper. It's too dangerous." But Aunt was determined, and for the next several days she worked until late in the evening with Comrade Kim and her followers.

Early one morning, Inchun and I heard Aunt chatting with the other Party members. "Comrades, I want to do more work for the Party. Communism is the way to go for us women. No men and no Japanese can tell us what to do anymore. I want to enlighten ignorant women and convert them to Marxism. The capitalistic Americans are no good. We must do what we can for Mother Russia." Comrade Kim, thoroughly delighted, immediately took Aunt Tiger to Natasha. Aunt Tiger told us later that they had a celebration to welcome her into the ranks.

Aunt Tiger quickly made friends with the Party leaders as well as with many of the frightened, timid towns-people. It did not take her long to know the real Reds from the Pinks. Between Kisa and Aunt Tiger we learned that there were many others looking to escape to the South.

As Aunt Tiger had hoped, she was able to get us a pro-ject that allowed us to work at home. We were given the task of making more flags and posters for our town. Mother and Inchun and I copied the propaganda slogans onto large banners and sewed flags at home all day long. The whole family had become trusted comrades and potential Party members.

Each day we waited for Father, fully prepared to leave for the South within minutes. For several nights after Kisa's visit, we lay awake listening for the urgent tap at the door. Our nervous anticipation turned to weary disappointment with the passing of the days. There was no sign of Father, and Aunt Tiger was having a harder and harder time pretending to be a devoted Party member. She produced no results as far as the Party was concerned. She had not identified any townspeople as traitors, nor had she brought any new members into the Party. And the Russians and Town Reds were beginning to keep an even closer eye on everyone. Party leaders had begun to issue passports to all of us. Even to cross the street I had to show my passport and have it stamped. Walks and visits were limited even within Kirimni.

At the Little Proletariat School, it grew increasingly difficult for me to listen to the awful propaganda and the constant harsh criticisms of the Capitalists. Anyone who was interested in anything other than the Marxist Red books was labeled a traitor and a Capitalist. We only talked about Mother Russia and the wonderful Communist leaders. I had to make the smaller children repeat after me: "We, the young proletarian comrades, are important. We can save our grown-up comrades from being Capitalists and Imperialists. If we see any comrades, whether father or mother, not understanding Mother Russia, we must report them to our comrade leader. This is our duty to Mother Russia. The Capitalists are our enemy. The Imperialists are our enemy. Mother Russia is for people like us. One for all and all for one. We are all equal and it is our duty to secure this social paradise."

It had been almost three weeks since Kisa had come.

As usual, I got dressed in my many layers of clothing in case that day would be the one. Inchun came to my room, and we watched the dawn breaking. The world seemed safe and peaceful. It was then that we heard footsteps outside the rice-paper paneled door. Our ears were so attuned to the atmosphere that no unusual sound or movement could escape our notice. We ran to the door. Mother and Aunt Tiger were already there, peering out into the semidarkness.

The door slid open and a foot entered awkwardly through the door. We knew it was Kisa. "It's okay. It's Kisa," he whispered with excitement. "I have a very special message from Uncle. He will not be able to come and get us. The security is too tight around here." Then he pulled out a small pouch of something and handed it to Mother as if it were some precious object. Carefully she untied the strings of the pouch. Rings and necklaces made of gold and jewels sparkled inside the handkerchief in which they were wrapped. Kisa said they were rare jewels and they would be enough to hire the best professional guide to help us cross the 38th Parallel. Kisa had made these arrangements over the past three days as Father had asked him to. The guide would come at exactly 4:30 in the morning, and would be dressed like a farmer, wearing straw shoes and carrying an A-frame on his back. Mother was to give the pouch to him before we left on the long journey.

"*You* give it to him when he comes. Why are you telling me this?" asked Mother.

Kisa sighed. "I can't go. If I disappear, the Russians will notice immediately and will send a search party after me. Then we'd all get caught and be brought back here to face the machine guns. Aunt Tiger and I have to be here to cover for you and give you a chance to cross the border. The two of us have been too visible. You must leave now and we will follow soon after. I have to run. Remember to be ready by four-thirty. That's when the patrol guards change shifts and the guide will want to use every minute of that time. So be waiting by the door, give him the pouch, and follow him immediately. He will be pleased with his pay, and he will treat you well, especially the little ones."

Aunt Tiger remained silent throughout all this. Mother turned to her in disbelief. "But both of you must come with us . . . "

Aunt Tiger did not respond, and Kisa simply said, "We will all see each other very soon. I must leave. Now, when you reach the South, there will be sources to help you locate your home in Seoul. That won't be a problem, so you needn't worry about that now." Kisa wished us a safe journey and lifted Inchun up onto his shoulder. He gave him a bounce, and put him down. Then he rested his hand on my head. I had always felt warm and secure in his presence. He hesitated for a second as if he wanted to say something special to me. I wished that he would come with us. Suddenly, I was gripped by the terrible fear that I would never see him again. I looked up at him and he smiled broadly to chase away the clouds of sadness within me. I could not smile back at him. He turned and slowly disappeared.

Mother looked deep into Aunt Tiger's eyes. But before Mother could speak, Aunt Tiger said, "I want to stay here, you know. I want to remain here until my husband comes back to me. I know he's not dead. He'll come back for me; he can't live without me."

"Maybe he went directly to the South from Japan. He probably heard the Russians were here and that many of the Northerners were escaping to the South. Maybe he is looking for you there . . . Why don't you come with us? Convince Kisa to come with us, too. We'll all risk it together."

Aunt Tiger took Mother's hands in hers and said resolutely, "Listen to me. All these years you were my strength. You were the one always helping me. I came to you as a bitter and spiteful woman whose only remaining objective in life was to get revenge on the Japanese for killing my parents and my babies and taking my home and husband from me. But thanks to you, look at me. I now have many people whom I love and most of all, I am able to help many people. I've found new purpose in life. This simple woman is going to do some good. I now know so many people who want to escape to the South. I want to help arrange a few more trips for the neighbors and then I will leave. It won't take too long."

Aunt Tiger left for her midnight Party meeting. As usual we draped thick blankets over our rice-paper paneled doors for fear that even the dim candlelight might attract the attention of the comrades. Mother told us to get some sleep. I lay awake filled with fear and anticipation. I watched the low candle burning, and listened to Mother walking about the dimly lit house. We were all afraid. So many things could go wrong. Once it was discovered that we were gone, the Communists would know that we had gone to the South. Kisa and Aunt Tiger would surely be suspected and punished. We had heard many cases of how those who were left behind were punished as traitors of Mother Russia. I tried to remember all that had happened today. It was too overwhelming to think that we were to escape without Kisa and Aunt Tiger. I could not imagine life without them. They were the family that I knew and loved. I knew them better than I knew my own father and brothers. I heard Inchun snoring softly beside me as we waited. My thoughts started to disperse into millions of bubbles. My entire body was suddenly overcome with exhaustion and I began to sleep.

When I woke up, I saw Aunt Tiger kneeling at the side of my bed. She must have just returned from the midnight Party meeting. She was smiling. She looked tenderly over at Inchun, and pulled his covers around him. "We will let him sleep a bit longer," she said. "I wanted to have a few moments with you before all the rushing about begins." Instead of saying anything special about our leaving each other, she started rummaging through her bag. She had brought some food from the Party meeting for our trip. Surely she was trying to hide her face as she searched for so long through her small bag. Her eyes were filling with tears. As Mother walked by, Aunt Tiger pulled out some money. "Keep it," she said. "Just in case something happens and you need it." Mother shook her head. Mother's eyes were closed and her lips were trembling. But Aunt Tiger insisted. "Please, I beg of you, let's not waste time talking about my coming along anymore." Mother looked down at the ground. Then she took the money and put it in the sock that she kept hidden under the long skirt of her *hanbok*, her *chima*.

It was hard to believe we were finally leaving Pyongyang. We were all ready. The guide was to arrive any minute. I went and sat with Inchun. We could hear the two grown-ups rushing about in the next room near the kitchen. It was windy and cold, and I listened to the rattle of the thin rice-paper paneled doors. I knew it was the last time I would hear the familiar sounds of our old house. I looked around the room. There were a few things I wished to take, but I knew I couldn't. If only I could take one of Grandfather's oxtail brushes with me.

Inchun and I must have somehow dozed off as we waited. Aunt Tiger came and tapped us awake and said, "He's here. Hurry." We followed her to Mother's room. Mother was dressed in dark clothes and had wrapped her head with a dark kerchief. The guide sat opposite her. He was a thin little man with a wrinkled leathery face baked by the sun. His small black eyes cast a strange light as he looked at us. In his rough chapped hands he held the pouch that Kisa had brought from Father. Next to him, propped against the wall was his A-frame.

The guide stood up, saying, "Good, you're ready. Children, remember, if you are stopped and questioned by anyone, I am your uncle. I came from Yohyun to fetch you in a hurry because your grandmother in Yohyun is dying. No matter how many times you are questioned, that is all you should say. Say you don't know anything else. You are children and you will get away with it. When we go through the checkpoint where they check passports, you stay behind me. The guards know me, because I live in the neighborhood and pass through often. They know I have many children. They'll probably just think you are mine. If your mother is pulled aside for questioning by the Russian soldiers, don't let them know she is your mother by making a scene. If all three of you are captured, the Russians will interrogate you separately and your mother probably won't make it. It'll be easier for your mother to make up some explanation if she's alone. As soon as they see a woman traveling with her children, they think she's up to something and start investigating. So, don't cry and call out to her. Don't even look back. Just follow me and march along casually. The soldiers will probably look your mother's passport over and let her go. She can catch up with us later."

While he spoke, Mother looked at us and when he was done, she said, "Remember to do exactly as he says." We understood. Mother said to the guide, "If for any reason I am detained and it looks as though it might take some time, please take care of the children. I put some extra money in the pouch for their use just in case. Perhaps you could take the children safely to the South first and come back for me." Then Mother looked at us and said, "Everything will be fine. Just listen and do as he says. We'll all be fine."

Aunt Tiger sat down beside us. "You needn't worry about these two children," she told the guide. "They are wiser than some old folks I know."

The guide slipped the pouch Mother had given him in his chest pocket underneath the many layers of strange clothing he was wearing. He strapped on his A-frame and headed toward the door. Aunt Tiger desperately reached out and grabbed our hands. Little Inchun burst out crying. Aunt Tiger hugged him and said, "Now, now, what is this? I'll be coming right after you." I saw Aunt Tiger wipe away her tears.

Mother gently pulled Inchun from Aunt Tiger and hugged him. "Don't make this any more difficult than it is," she whispered to him. "Everything will be fine, you'll see." Meanwhile, the guide was waiting impatiently outside the door. He made a hissing noise like a cat to get us to hurry. We left Aunt Tiger standing in the yard staring out into the darkness. It was strange to leave this house where I had lived all my life. It was strange to leave everything I loved. Inchun had not even taken his little top. We were allowed to take nothing but a small snack and our passports. The guide took the passports from us and Mother kept hers. We did not question him. He was the leader. He knew the Russian soldiers' rules and schedules, just as he knew which streets were safe and when. Our lives depended on him. We had to obey him unconditionally. Yet I feared we had entrusted our lives to a greedy farmer.

Mother held our hands. The guide walked so fast that we had to run to keep sight of him as he wove through the small back roads of Kirimni leading to the train station. Often we heard the barks of the Russian guard dogs patrolling the main streets. At this, we would stand perfectly still until we heard the barking fade into the distance. The guide did not look back once to see if we were following him.

We chased after him for two hours in fear that we might lose him. The cold, gray morning light was greeting us. I could see the train station in the distance. Now we were out in a wide street and had joined a crowd of people heading toward the station. Farmers and peddlers were bringing their wares to sell to the passengers on the train. Many of the people at the station looked as if they had slept there. Perhaps they had missed the midnight train. Many had cages of chickens and rabbits, or crates of food with them. I suddenly noticed that the guide had disappeared.

I nudged Mother and she whispered, "Don't say anything, just stay next to me. He knows what he is doing." We sat on the cold concrete and waited. Inchun just listened and did not say a thing. His pale little face was still streaked with the tears he had shed when we left Aunt.

The Russian soldiers and North Korean police, with their guns flung over their shoulders, were walking around the station scrutinizing everyone. Mother pushed my head down into her lap and closed my eyes with her hands. We sat quietly amidst the hundreds of other passengers who were waiting for the train. I wondered how many of these ragged farmers and peasants were headed to the South as we were. They looked gloomy and tired, with their heads between their knees, hoping to avoid the attention of the police. It was safest to look like all the others and blend into the crowd. The police and the soldiers lifted several of the sleepy faces only to let them drop back down. They wove through the crowds practically stepping on people's legs and hands.

A big boot stepped between Inchun and me, almost crushing my hand. The hem of the man's heavy khaki coat brushed against my face. It smelled awful, and left me feeling afraid. Up close, the guns looked even bigger than I had thought. I was supposed to keep my head down and my eyes closed, but I followed the police with my eyes. They must have been looking for someone. Mother pushed my head back down again, and she rested her hand on my head to make sure I would not look around. After a while the police went away. The guide reappeared and sat at the opposite corner of the station. He put his A-frame down, leaned against it, and went to sleep.

Finally, the train arrived. The station became chaotic as people got off the train and stepped through the crowd. Most of them were farmers who had come to sell their wares at the station or at the Pyongyang city market. They carried big bundles of fresh eggs and corn, live chickens, and handicrafts. The smell of steamed corn and sweet rice cakes filled the air. The women balanced big baskets on their heads, and some had babies strapped to their backs. The vendors called out to the crowds, trying to sell their goods, and some of the people who had been sleeping and waiting around the train station for so long got up to buy food.

Mother didn't buy anything. We had to rush to the train to follow our guide. I wished we had a minute to buy one of those steaming ears of sweet corn. I was hungry and cold. But Mother took us by the hand and led us along. The station was so crowded that we were pushed by the swarms of people moving toward the train. Mother was constantly on the look-out for our guide, while holding tightly to us. The masses of people parted only for the armed police or the soldiers. Pushing and squeezing to make room where there was none, some people cried out in pain or fell and were stepped on. Mother lifted Inchun and carried him so that he would not be crushed or separated from us. There were too many people. The train was already full. By the time we were pushed onto the train, we had lost sight of the guide. I could see the anxious look on Mother's face as she searched in all directions.

There **were** no seats or windows. I heard people say the Japanese had broken all the windows and removed the seats before they left. The cold wind blew through the cars. None of this mattered, though. We were desperate to find our guide. We were completely lost without him. We hadn't even realized that the train was already well on its way. People began to settle down. Some were able to stake out a small space on the floor to sit. We huddled together on the floor, trying to dodge the damp night air. Mother kept looking around while trying not to attract the attention of the secret police, who seemed to be hiding everywhere.

I don't know how long we sat on the cold floor of that crowded train. My whole body ached. I wanted to stand up and stretch my legs, but Mother said that if I stood up, there might not be enough room for me to sit again. At least all the bodies pressed against each other helped us stay a little warmer. But Inchun, cold, hungry, and uncomfortable, began to sob. He had a stomachache and vomited. People made rude remarks and stood up. I was glad when they stood because they now served as shields against the wind.

As we crossed over the Daedong River for the last time, I realized how silly I was to have thought that I would be able to say goodbye to it. I loved the Daedong River. I remembered taking walks along its banks when I was little. Those times seemed so far away it was almost like a fairy tale.

The packages of food that Aunt had packed were now lost. It didn't matter. The train smelled so awful I couldn't have eaten anyway. I closed my eyes as the rickety train rattled along while the rain and wind came rushing in on us.

After what seemed like an eternity, Mother pulled us up gently. It was our turn to get off the train. I couldn't see the guide. Perhaps Mother had caught sight of him or had received special instructions before we left. We walked with the crowd, relieved to be off the train. Up ahead I thought I saw our guide with the A-frame on his back.

All I could see for miles were rice paddies and fields. On a narrow mud walkway between the rice paddies, some of the others who had gotten off the train with us were walking single file toward a little house that must be the checkpoint for passports. The guide was far in front of us. I was walking behind an old man, Inchun was right behind me, and Mother was in the rear.

It wasn't raining anymore. The setting sun cast a pinkish glow on the long line of people ahead of us and created a wave-like shadow on the empty fields. The corn had been cut and the rice harvested. Save for a few bales of hay, the fields were bare. I kept looking back to make sure Inchun and Mother were behind me. After a long walk, we finally reached the guardhouse where many people were lined up, waiting to have their passports checked. Mother looked worried and she shot a disapproving glance at me whenever I looked back at her. The line was long and we moved forward very slowly.

We waited and waited, gradually drawing closer and closer. I saw our guide pass safely through and begin walking down the road away from the guardhouse. When it was my turn, nobody even asked me anything. The three

Russian soldiers, with their guns and dogs close by, were too busy looking at the passports of the grown-ups. One of them motioned for me to get out of the way. He was much more interested in seeing Mother's passport. He stretched out his hand for her papers. As we had been instructed, Inchun and I kept walking.

When I finally turned to look for Mother, expecting her to be close behind us, I saw that she was still standing at the guardhouse. A Korean soldier in his red-brimmed hat was looking at her passport. He handed it over to a Russian soldier. I saw them pull Mother out of line. Inchun and I stood frozen as we watched. I could tell she saw me and was worried. She shot a glance at me. I remembered what the guide had said, and knew Mother was trying to tell me to go on.

"Mommy, Mommy, Mommy," Inchun sobbed. At this, I suddenly came to, told him to hush, and pulled him by the arm, hoping no one had heard. To my surprise, Inchun started crying louder than ever and dragging his feet. I practically had to drag him along as I hurried to catch up with the guide, who was rapidly disappearing from sight.

"Don't you remember what Mother and the guide said? You'll get Mother in more trouble if you don't stop. We have to move on and wait for her where the Russians won't see us. She'll come and join us soon. Mother wants us to go. I looked back at her again and I could tell by the way she looked at us." Inchun kept crying. He said nothing and the swollen tears came streaming down his cheeks. I cried, too. I didn't know what to think or say anymore, but we had to keep going.

We ran and caught up with the guide. All those people who had stood in line at the passport checkpoint had disappeared. The only person I saw was our guide in front of us. Without turning to look at us, the guide yelled through clenched teeth, "If you children keep sobbing like that, the soldiers will suspect something and keep your mother longer. Be quiet, and she will be released soon and will join us at that little house. She knows where to find you. Just follow me and don't look back." He walked faster and faster.

I looked back, despite his warning. The little wooden guardhouse, the soldiers, and my mother were small specks in the distance. I couldn't see much of anything anyway, for my eyes were filled with tears. I was afraid I would never see my mother again. Inchun kept crying as if she were dead. I had never seen him cry like this and it scared me. He tried not to make noise, and his muffled sobs racked his entire body. He rubbed his eyes with his dirty little fingers, leaving dark stains on his cheeks. I squeezed his hands and whispered, "Mother will join us soon. For now we have to catch up with the guide. We can't afford to lose him. He is the only person we know in this strange town."

Inchun and I were tired, hungry, and cold. It was getting dark, and we could hardly see the shadowy figure hurrying on ahead of us. We began to fall behind. My shoes were wet and my feet were frozen. My stomach growled with hunger. Little Inchun was still crying. I stopped to comfort him and picked him up to carry him on my back. His tears fell on my neck. After I carried him for a while, he fell asleep. Only then did I realize how heavy he was. I had given him piggyback rides before, but I had never realized he was this heavy.

The guide, who had seemed so heartless, finally stopped to wait for us. When he saw me wobbling under the weight, and sinking into the mud, he uttered his first kind words to me. "A sleeping child is very heavy. Wake him up and let him walk. As soon as we cross this little hill, there will be a small inn where your mother will join us. She may already be there if she took the short cut. Then we can make the final part of the journey to the South." Inchun had awakened and heard the part about the short cut. He stopped crying and jumped down. We walked quickly, keeping our eyes on the hill ahead of us. It wasn't a little hill as the guide had said. It looked more like a mountain. We continued on in silence.

Swallowed by the darkness, we climbed up the steep path. I saw the crescent moon coming over the mountain to greet us, and I pointed it out to Inchun. As we started heading down the hill, we saw a small, dimly lit, thatched-roof house. An old woman and several men were sitting around, smoking long pipes. Our guide told us to go inside and ask the woman about our mother. He said he would be back for all of us later.

We went ahead and were met with curious glances. A toothless, wrinkled old woman approached us and asked whether that man was our guide. Too tired to think what I should say, I nodded. She sighed and took us into the house. She gave us food and watched us gobble up her vegetables and rice as she puffed on her long pipe. She then told us to go to sleep. We asked about Mother, but the old lady said, "Just sleep. Perhaps she is on her way."

Inchun started to cry again. I was not prepared to cope with this lost child who constantly cried for Mother. Gone was the wise old man that Mother always said lived inside that little boy's body. It seemed that the wise old man left Inchun's body when Mother was pulled aside by the Russian soldier at the passport checkpoint. Inchun cried himself to sleep. With his tear-streaked face, he looked like a little angel whose wings had been clipped. I thought to myself, I must find Mother . . . soon, very soon, for Inchun. Otherwise, he will cry himself to death. I soon drifted off into a delicious forgetful sleep, and dreamed that Mother would be next to me when I awoke.

A chilly draft, a bony hand on my shoulder, and the voice of the old woman telling me to wake up made me jump. In the still gray morning, her urgent words fell on me like a hammer, dashing my last hope. She said we must be up and on our way before the soldiers came by for their inspection. We must return to the train station and go back home. She couldn't bear to tell us last night that the guide we hired was a double agent. He regularly informed the soldiers about his catch and they paid him a fee. The old lady said Mother would not be coming to join us and we would only bring harm to the people in her inn. We must leave and catch the morning train home, she said. She felt sorry for us, but she couldn't keep us anymore.

Inchun listened wide-eyed, as he scratched the mosquito bites on his arms and legs until they started to bleed. The mosquitoes had made a feast of his little body. Even his eyelids were swollen. I too was covered with bloody patches. We must have scratched ourselves all night.

The woman gave us some food wrapped in a cotton handkerchief and told us to follow the road to the train station. We couldn't miss it. Since it was market day, it wouldn't be unusual to see children walking through the village. The old lady said there were many secret agents in Yohyun out to catch "traitors" like us who did not like the rules of Mother Russia. We must be careful whom we talked to.

No mother, no money, no passport, I thought to myself. How are we supposed to go anywhere? So many thoughts went reeling through my head. I sat up and tears filled my eyes. I felt lost and abandoned. I didn't know what to do. My head ached and the tears streamed down my face like a heavy rain.

Then a timid hand crept into my wet palm and waited to be held. I hugged my brother tightly and cried, "Inchun, Inchun, I'm sorry, I'm sorry, I'm sorry . . . I just don't know what to do anymore, I don't know anymore . . ."

To my great surprise, he pulled away and, holding my two hands in his little hands, said, "*Nuna,* you can't cry like this. Big sisters don't cry. You are my *nuna.* I'll always obey you because you are my *nuna.* I'm sorry I cried so much asking for Mother. I won't cry anymore. Let's go and look for Mother. Maybe she's still at that guardhouse. Let's tell the soldiers to give our mother back to us. Or maybe she'll be at the train station. Let's go." I was stunned to hear my little brother taking charge like this. It was hard to believe that this was the same little Inchun who had cried all day yesterday.

We thanked the kind old woman, and she smiled and wished us luck. I thought her toothless smile and wrinkled face looked pretty against the rising sun. Her bony fingers, yellowed from crushing tobacco leaves for her pipe, felt comforting when she patted my mosquito-bitten head.

Inchun and I left hand in hand. No one else seemed to be around. The old lady stood in the doorway, her long pipe resting comfortably on her thin lower lip. Blowing smoke rings into the morning air, she watched us go down the road.

Chapter Nine

We walked, hand in hand, silently down the hill toward the rising sun. On so peaceful a morning, we were hopeful that something good would happen. My feet and calves ached from walking so long and so quickly the day before. My mosquito bites were burning and itching. Inchun, after his sudden outburst that morning, had retreated into silence. He didn't complain about his feet or the mosquito bites. He just limped along, stopping only to scratch himself. All of a sudden, he pointed his thin little finger toward a long snake-like object winding through the cluster of trees and brown mountains. Maybe Mother is on that train, I thought. We quickened our pace and went down the hill.

We continued, chewing on the rice balls that the old lady had given us, but we were getting very thirsty. At the foot of the hill was the village marketplace, where women had come to sell food: hard-boiled eggs, rice cakes, bean cakes, and sweet persimmon juice. Others brought fabric, baskets, and the like. Women of all shapes and sizes carried wares in baskets on their heads. Some had children strapped to their backs. The sun was beating down upon us, and Inchun and I were perspiring in the many layers of clothing we were wearing. There were no trees to offer their shade, and so we kept wandering through the market. "Fresh, steaming hot corn," one woman called out. "Large eggs, the best deal in the market. Over here!" Inchun and I looked carefully at each woman, peering up at each face shadowed by a basket. We thought Mother might be in the marketplace disguised as a peddler while she searched for us. Discouraged, we turned to make our way toward the guardhouse.

As we wandered down the hill, we passed a thin woman with a big basket on her head; a chubby child strapped to her back was twisting and turning in an attempt to free himself. The woman's sun-baked face was perspiring heavily as she tried to balance her wares with one hand and soothe the unhappy child with the other. It looked as if the baby had been in that position for a long time. My first thought was how lucky that baby was to be so close to his mother, but then I felt sorry for the harassed woman. She needed to get up the hill and spread out her wares, as all the other ladies had, in order to make some money.

I went up to her and offered to watch her baby. The woman looked us over, thought about it for a while, and then stooped to put down her basket. She untied the wide strip of cotton material which she used to tie the baby to her body. The baby immediately let out a scream of joy and went running. We chased after him while his mother tied the cotton belt back around her waist. Reveling in her newfound freedom, her arms swung back and forth as she practically sprinted up the hill, anxious to get her day's work started. Now and then, she stopped to look back to make sure we were taking good care of her baby.

By the time we got up the hill, she had already set out her basket of freshly steamed corn. She must have had the ears well wrapped, for there was still some steam rising from the sweet yellow kernels. Inchun and I stayed close by, playing with the plump little child. We might all have been taken for her children. The woman sold all her corn very quickly and said she wanted to go home and get more to sell before the market day was over. Thanking us, she offered us each a big ear of corn that she had saved for us. How delicious it was after having smelled the sweet steam for so long. This ear of corn was to be our lunch and dinner, for we had no money.

We walked along many of the same roads we had traveled the day before. It was late afternoon when we finally reached the train station. The platform was empty and I noticed for the first time what a small station it was. We went inside and sat on a small corner bench, resting our feet, full of cuts and blisters. Suddenly, an old man with a broom came out of nowhere and started to sweep the floors. Starting in the far corner, he slowly worked his way toward us. With his eyes fixed on the little mound of dirt and rubbish, he asked, "Did you lose someone trying to go to the South?"

"We lost our mother," I replied. "Did you see a tall, skinny, pretty lady looking for her two children?" Inchun turned and stared at me. I probably should not have told the man all of this information, but I was so relieved to come upon someone who seemed to understand our plight. I was too tired to think anymore.

Without lifting his head, the man continued to sweep and softly said he had not seen anyone nor could he help us now. "You can't stay here. The police come by all the time. You better go now," he urged.

We reluctantly left the little bench and wandered around. Eventually, we found a barn and went inside. It was empty except for a large pile of hay. My stomach was growling, and my muscles ached. Inchun rested his head against me, and began dozing. I decided to rest and look for Mother the next morning.

I heard strange noises outside the barn. I tried not to fall asleep as I was determined to keep guard for Inchun. Clutching my muddy sneakers as ammunition, I stayed up most of the night. Grateful for the hay that kept us warm, I passed the time by counting our mosquito bites. Inchun and I had bites and scabs covering our legs, arms, and faces, and I realized that we must look as if we had some awful disease.

Dawn was breaking when Inchun awoke. Driven by hunger, we decided to head for the only place where we knew we would be safe and might be able to earn a meal for ourselves. We marched up the long stretch of road to the marketplace, and hoped to find the lady with the baby. We had to stop often because our feet ached, and tears filled our eyes as we made ourselves press on. We were grateful for the warm sun, which helped take the sting out of our mosquito bites. It was almost noon by the time we made it to the marketplace. To our great relief, we found the lady with the chubby little baby. He was pounding on his mother's back with his fat fists, crying and thrashing about to loosen the wide belt that bound him. His mother tried to ignore him and was calling out, "Sweet, steaming hot corn, fresh hot corn." Seeing us, she put the baby down. We kept our distance as we played with the baby, for I was afraid that if people saw how dirty and sickly Inchun and I looked, they would not buy corn from her. The lady gave us more corn than the day before. Though we saw many new faces as we sat playing with the baby, we couldn't find our mother.

For three days Inchun and I searched for Mother near the marketplace, sleeping in the barn each night and surviving on the corn that we earned by babysitting. On the fourth day we went back to the train station hoping to run into the old man with the broom. We sat on the bench nervously watching for the police, and suddenly heard the brushing of a broom. As he drew near, we looked at him. He did not look at us, but he said in a low voice as he continued to sweep, "You children are still here? Come back here late in the afternoon. We will figure out what to do. You can't stay here like this." Then he disappeared.

After we rested for a while, we looked at each other

and were both sure we were ready to face the soldiers. We could never find Mother alone, so we decided to take the risk. We held hands and walked in the direction of the wooden guardhouse where they had pulled Mother aside. We could see it in the distance, and knew it would be a long walk through the rice paddies. Finally, we arrived. We peeked through a side door and saw two Russian soldiers. Two dogs were lazily sleeping next to them. No one was threatened by us; no one even knew we were there. Not even the dogs wanted to get up for us.

The soldiers were talking, humming, and munching on a long loaf of dark bread. Their mighty machine guns were resting against the wall within arm's reach. Their red-brimmed hats lay on the table. These soldiers both had hair on their heads, and did not look as savage as the Kirimni soldiers with their shaven heads. I decided that they looked as if they might help me find Mother.

As a *nuna* I had to make the decisions and do all the talking. I looked at Inchun, who quietly stared down at his feet, waiting for his big sister to decide what to do next. I was ready to act, but I still did not know quite how to approach them. All of a sudden one of the soldiers poked his head out and said, *"Kara!"* meaning "Go away!" in Korean.

I blurted out, "We want to know what you did with our mother. We came to get her." I stared into his eyes and I didn't move. I was frightened. I could see out of the corner of my eye the guns and the dogs inside the guardhouse. Hearing my voice, the dogs lazily opened their eyes, only to close them again. Again I asked what they had done with Mother. By this time Inchun was squeezing my hand so tightly I thought he would break my fingers. But we stood with our chins held high trying to appear very brave.

The man looked at us standing hand in hand gripped with determination, and a faint smile crept across his face. He called out to the other soldier who was tearing off a bite of bread. The younger soldier's eyes were blue like the sky, a deep cobalt blue. He reminded me of Ivan Malenkiv, the first Russian soldier I had ever met. I thought maybe this soldier with the same clear blue eyes would like us and would help us.

After a few minutes, the older one made a face and turned away, looking bored. But the younger soldier invited us in. He spoke a bit of Korean, but said many words that I couldn't quite understand. Gesticulating, he pointed to us and then to himself, and I understood that he had a little sister and brother like us at home in his country. He gave us some of his dark bread. Though coarse, it was chewy and delicious to us after eating nothing but steamed corn for three days. We ate in silence, relieved that he was so friendly, but still afraid of what might happen to us. His large blue eyes gazed gently at us as we ate, and he began to seem like a friend.

I asked him once again, "Can you tell me where you are keeping my mother? We want to find our mother. We lost her here almost four days ago. Can you find her for us?"

He didn't answer. Instead, he lifted Inchun up on his lap, gave him more bread, and pointing to himself, said, "Dobraski, Dobraski." Inchun repeated "Dobraski," and the soldier laughed heartily.

The other soldier started shouting at Dobraski in Russian. He pointed to us and then to a big brick building far off in the distance. The dogs began to growl at us. Dobraski shouted at them and they quieted down at once. Dobraski shouted something to the older soldier, who gruffly shouted back at him. The older one picked up his gun, grabbed the dogs by their leashes, and walked off. Dobraski said nothing. He suddenly stood up, picked up his machine gun, swung it over his shoulder, and pointing to the jeep parked in the distance, motioned for us to follow. He was angry. I wondered what would happen now. Inchun and I followed him in silence.

I had seen hundreds and hundreds of these jeeps in Pyongyang but I had never ridden in one. I got in reluctantly, but Inchun was clearly excited to be sitting in the front. Dobraski hopped in and proceeded to drive down the muddy road. The cold air was refreshing and my dirty hair flew in the breeze.

Before I knew it, the jeep had stopped in front of the brick building with the big red Russian flag fluttering in the wind. Dobraski took us inside. It was clean and smelled like a paper factory. On every desk, there were huge stacks of papers, and we could hardly see the soldiers sitting behind these desks. One of the soldiers talked to Dobraski and then took us into a big, empty room.

While we sat waiting, I said quietly to Inchun, "If they take us in separately and ask lots of questions, just say that you don't know anything. Just say that all you know is that we were going to see our grandmother in Yohyun. Tell them I know everything."

Inchun stared wide-eyed at me, and nodded. He started to sob. He was exhausted and frightened. I felt like crying, too, but I told Inchun it would be all right. I didn't believe it myself, and I wondered if that was how Mother had felt all those times.

After a while, a Korean Communist soldier with red epaulets and a red cap came in. He looked very stern and official. "You are the children who went to the guard-house and asked for your mother?" We nodded. He was cold and mean-looking and I didn't like him. He stared closely at us, then pointed to Inchun and said, "You, follow me."

Inchun looked at me and I said, "I am his *nuna* and we go everywhere together. Can I come, too?"

Glaring at me, he replied, "I will call you when I need you."

Inchun's face grew pale as he followed the soldier into the next room. I wondered what he was going to do to little Inchun. I sat in the empty room wondering whether someone was going to come and question me, too. Was someone watching me right now? I had heard horrible stories about Communist interrogation techniques. People in our town said they were merciless with those who tried to escape to the South. My stomach ached and I held my tummy and rested my head on my knees.

After what seemed like days, Inchun came out and said, "They want you to go in right now. They told me not to talk to you. Are you sick, *Nuna?*" Inchun was still very pale, but he seemed to be all right otherwise.

I didn't answer. I just shook my head and went into the next room. As soon as I entered, the Korean Communist soldier shut the door and pointed to the hard wooden chair in front of a large desk piled high with official-looking documents. Behind the desk was a stout, bespectacled Russian officer. He asked my father's name and I told him. He asked me where my father was. I told him I had not seen him for many years as he had fled to Manchuria to avoid being imprisoned by the Japanese. He asked me if I had any big brothers and if I knew where they were. I told him I had three older brothers, but that I had not seen them for a long time either, as they were taken to labor camps by the Japanese soldiers and did not come home after the war. I was so frightened that it was not until then that I realized he was speaking to me in fluent Korean. Then he asked me why I was so far from my home in Pyongyang and what had happened to my passport. At this I started to say exactly what our guide had told us. I told him we were on our way to visit our sick grandmother. I was not in the habit of lying so I started to mumble. I hesitated when I tried to explain that my grandmother lived right near the border. All of a sudden, the Korean Communist officer shouted at me, "Tell the truth!" He struck the table with his fist. I was so startled that I started to cry.

The Russian officer looked disturbed and said something in Russian to the other officer, who then left the room. I was glad that he made that mean-looking Korean Communist leave. As the man left, he pushed my head with his large hand and said, "You'd better tell the truth to our Comrade Major." This young Communist reminded me of many eager young Korean men I had seen in Pyongyang who espoused Communism. They seemed more dedicated to Mother Russia than the Russians themselves. They were more anxious to kill traitors like me and my family than the Russians were. They had no sympathy for us as their fellow countrymen. To them, the idea of becoming a dedicated Communist comrade was more important. It came as no surprise to me that the Comrade Major was less ominous.

He was a soft-spoken man. He also had red epaulets, but in addition had several red patches emblazoned on the front of his uniform. Looking at me, he said that he could not find my mother. It would be best for us to go back home to our relatives.

I mustered all my courage and said, "Please find my mother. She was taken by one of your soldiers at the checkpoint."

He told me he knew all about it and if he saw her he would tell her to go home just as he was now telling me.

Then he let me sit there while he did his paperwork. He was looking through the many papers he had with photographs of Koreans pasted in the corner. I sat quietly, hoping he would say something about my mother. Maybe one of those papers was hers. After a long while, he called to a soldier who must have been standing outside the door. He said something to the soldier, who then led me and Inchun out the door and told us to go away.

Inchun and I felt completely lost and just stood outside that cold gray building. It had seemed a short distance from the guardhouse when we rode in the jeep, but now the checkpoint looked like a little pea in the distance. We walked in silence. I saw a large warehouse and I thought I heard noises coming from inside. Two armed soldiers were marching back and forth in front of the building with their dogs. I wondered if Mother was being held there. Was there something we had said that might make them hurt Mother? I felt miserable and I was glad Inchun didn't ask me any questions. We continued on toward the guardhouse. We could try asking Dobraski one last time.

After a long, tiresome walk, we reached the little guardhouse, where we found Dobraski humming a familiar Russian tune. Before I even had the chance to say anything, he pointed in the direction of the train station and then at the setting sun. We understood that he wanted us to go before dark. He went back inside. He didn't want us around anymore.

Lost and alone, Inchun and I reached for each other's hands and walked slowly toward the station. It was getting dark and chilly. We saw Dobraski peek out from the guardhouse to watch us as we passed the other soldier walking up and down the path with the two dogs. The dogs seemed to know us and didn't bark at us. I dropped a lump of the dark bread Dobraski had given me in front of the dogs. I wanted them to know that I liked them.

I thought of Dobraski in his khaki uniform with the red patches signifying his rank, his black boots that came all the way up to his knees, and the familiar gun he had slung about him. He resembled other Russian soldiers I had seen, but somehow he seemed different. I wished we could have stayed with him until we found Mother. I felt certain that she was being held somewhere around there. Maybe Dobraski knew something about her whereabouts, but was powerless to do anything. I looked back many times to see if he would ask us to return, but he didn't.

We continued walking toward the station along the narrow path between the rice paddies. I thought of Mother. If Mother were still in the hands of the Russians, maybe she would be lucky enough to meet someone as nice as Dobraski and the major. But maybe Mother was already in the South, having assumed that the guide had taken care of us as she had asked. We had never expected to be lost like this, and so we had never discussed what to do. I knew we could never go home to Kirimni. Traitors like us would be shot to death. Aunt and Kisa would be shot, too, for taking us in.

I looked at Inchun. I didn't feel like talking, but I hoped he might prattle on about something as my head was aching from trying to think about what we should do next. I was tired and hungry and wanted to eat the rest of the dark bread that Dobraski had given us. But I had hidden it under my skirt, knowing we had a long way ahead of us and had to conserve our supply to survive.

Inchun started to cry and ask for the food. He tugged at my skirt, and kept crying, "Nuna, I'm hungry. Let me have some bread now." I told him he had to wait. Inchun asked again for the bread and I told him to wait until we were really hungry. "Now, Nuna, I am really hungry now!" Inchun cried, tugging at my skirt. He was like any other tired, cranky, hungry little boy. I felt sad and completely alone. But at the same time I was annoyed at myself for expecting so much from him. I gave him the rest of the bread. "Chew it for a long time and eat slowly so you won't get a stomachache," I warned. He ate in silence, holding my hand and lagging as far behind me as his little arm could stretch.

Chapter Ten

When we arrived at the small country train station, it was much too late to expect to find the old man who said he would help us. Since it was almost dark, we walked around the station to see if it would be safe for us to spend the night. A few people passed by without even looking at us. Everyone was afraid of being spotted by the police. We saw some soldiers walking by, talking and laughing loudly. We sat down on the wooden floor facing the little ticket booth that was closed. Inchun complained about a stomachache just as I had feared, and cried himself to sleep on my lap. I didn't know if we would even see the man with the broom, and he was our only hope.

My bones ached, and I suddenly realized how exhausted I was. For the past three days I had dragged my tired feet up and down so many long country roads. I was covered with mud from going through the rice paddies at all hours. I had often given Inchun piggyback rides and my feet had sunk deep into the wet earth. As a result, my ankles and legs were caked with many different shades of mud. It was hard to be a *nuna*. I wished someone older than I were around. I didn't like being the older one, though I loved Inchun and I wanted to take care of him. I was tired and I cried as I caressed his dirty hair, stiff from the mud and rain. We had not been able to wash or bathe since we left Pyongyang, and we were both dirty and smelly and covered with bruises and scabs from the mosquito bites.

Consumed with hunger and exhaustion, I too must have dozed off and slept. Suddenly, startled by a noise, I awoke. It was the old man with the broom. He motioned for us to follow. I shook Inchun and we went with the man to the corner of the train station by his broom closet. He said, "I was waiting for you for the earlier train, but you were not here."

"I am sorry, sir. We were talking to the Russian guards hoping they would help us find our mother."

He looked startled, shook his head in disbelief, and said, "Look, many people in this town have seen you, so you'd better get going. It's not safe for you here. The Russian soldiers take children away. We don't know what they do with little children, but they do disappear. You are very daring and have been very lucky. Maybe your mother is already in the South. Do you have relatives in the South?"

"Yes."

"Good, I don't think you have much choice anyway. You've come this far. You have to go just a bit further to cross the Thirty-eighth Parallel. Then things will be better for you. You won't have to live in fear when you're old like me. No time to waste." The old man did not expect any response from us. He pulled out an old ticket stub. "Here, take this and don't lose it," he said. "When the night train arrives, there will be two conductors in the station, one young and one old. You make sure you line up on the far right where the old fellow is; he's a friend of mine. You give this stub to him and he will see to it that you get a chance to cross to the other side of the tracks." By this time, I was so confused and scared that I was ready to say, "Maybe we should go back to Pyongyang and see if my aunt can help us. Maybe I can go home." The old man looked at my helpless stare and sighed, as he said, "Come, I will show you what I mean."

He went to the little window at the station. He made sure no one was coming and then whispered, "You have to get to the other side of the tracks and then go down the hill. Do you see that cornfield in the distance?" We nodded and he quickly continued, "Walk through that cornfield, but you have to look out for the search beam. When you see a bright beam, sit down and don't move. Wait until it goes away, then continue walking. After you get through the cornfield, do you see that little hill?" The old man looked at me with urgency. I was not sure, because it was rather dark already, but I thought I saw a dark mass behind the cornfield, so I nodded. "Go up and over that hill. It has many trees and it should be safe. Once you get over the hill you can see the barbed-wire fence. That fence is the Thirty-eighth Parallel. Run with all your might until you get to the barbed-wire fence and go under it. You are little and can crawl under. Don't stop for anything. Once you are on the other side of the fence, you will be in the South and you will be free. Maybe your mother is already there, waiting for her brave little ones."

He looked as if he himself wanted to risk it. I felt like saying, "Will you come with us?" But he fell silent and looked worried. He reached deep into the pocket of his old wrinkled trousers and took out a small package wrapped in an old handkerchief. "Here, take this. Munch on these while you wait for the search beam to pass over you."

I felt flushed with relief, and was very grateful to this old man, but instead of thanking him, I said, "But, the train will be here. How do we get to the other side of the tracks without being caught?"

The old man said, "The old conductor will look after you, just watch him carefully when you give him the ticket and follow his directions. Don't worry, he'll know I sent you. Just make sure you give him the ticket." He then disappeared as he saw some people approaching the station.

I was gripped with fear as I saw our only friend slip into the darkness. I wanted to follow him home and wash up, and eat, and rest for the night. I could picture him going back to a small house with a low thatched roof, and warm gray smoke swirling up from the chimney into the dark night sky. His sweet old wife was probably waiting for him with some hot soup. He was a kind man and had put himself at great risk to help us. It was then I smelled the sweetness of rice cakes from the package he had given me. I was ashamed I never thanked him for his kindness.

To my surprise, people started coming from all directions and before I knew it, the station was filled with silent shadows. No one spoke. They lined up and waited for the train. After a while, two conductors came out and started rattling their ticket punchers. We waited until we saw the elderly conductor heading toward the right side of the platform, then we followed him and got in line. We heard the train screeching and lurching to a stop. My stomach churned and my throat burned with fear. What if the old conductor gets caught trying to help us? What if he is not the right old conductor? What if he doesn't know about us?

The young conductor was asking for some people's passports. The older man was also looking at many people's passports and asking where they were going. Finally, it was our turn. I stretched out my arm to give him the ticket and looked up at him. He looked at us, punched our used ticket, and whispered, "To the end of the train." Pushing us on our way, he said loudly, "Next, next, passport, please."

I grabbed Inchun's hand and started walking to the end of the platform. People were pouring off the train, pushing and shoving through the crowds. As we got farther down the platform, the crowds started thinning out. It seemed awkward not to get on the train, and I was afraid we would be noticed. I looked back to see if anyone was staring, and saw the old conductor walking behind us. He bellowed, "All vendors must get back on the train now. You can sell your things at the next stop." Then I realized that the women with baskets in their arms were selling steamed potatoes and boiled eggs to the people getting on and off. The women grabbed their things quickly and went running onto the train.

Inchun and I had almost reached the last compartment when the old conductor drew closer behind us and started talking to a straggling vendor still trying to make a few more sales. "You must get on the train, now." Then he whispered to us, "I'll shield you from view. Quickly, crawl underneath the train, and when you're on the other side of the tracks, run down the hill just part way. Stay put until you see the train pull away. Then you can run to the bottom of the hill and cross the field."

The conductor looked around and squatted over as if to pick something up. Inchun and I bent down and crawled under the train. The vibration of the tracks was scary and the metal felt cold as I grabbed onto part of the wheel to steady myself while Inchun clung to me. We crawled out the other side of the train and ran a little way down the hill and crouched down until the train pulled away.

The dark cornfield up ahead seemed to be harboring all sorts of evil creatures and I imagined them whispering, "Go back to the old man and stay with him. You won't make it through here." I looked at the package I was clutching, opened it, and gave a rice cake to Inchun. He ate in silence and I knew he was swallowing his tears as he ate. We waited a long time, squatting against the pebbly hill. The pale moon was high above us, but dark clouds soon covered its light. It was damp, and chills ran through me like sharp little needles. I reached out and hugged Inchun, hoping to warm us both. I wanted to walk down the hill and get to the cornfield, but I was afraid of the searchlight. I wanted to see what it looked like before we started on our way.

Inchun shivered and said, "*Nuna*, how long are we going to sit here like this? These little stones are hurting me and I have to lock my knees and dig my heels in to keep from sliding. My legs are getting tired already."

I knew what he meant. I realized that I, too, was holding myself up by digging my heels into the dirt, and my calves were aching. "We will run down soon, but I just want to know what the searchlight is like. All the cornstalks are cut short. They won't hide us very well."

Inchun sat quietly and then exclaimed, "Look, look over there! It's like a rainbow. Look how it moves." He pointed to the left side of the field and then to the right. I saw a bright greenish-colored beam covering the ground.

The search beam passed over the cornfield and then passed near us as we sat crouched very still. Then, Inchun and I looked at each other, grabbed each other's hands, and started to run and slide the rest of the way to the cornfield. The pebbles that we dislodged as we ran came tumbling down the hill, making a hissing noise as they scraped against each other. We fell and ended up rolling part of the way down. It hurt as the pebbles dug into us, but we were glad to be at the foot of the hill. We stopped at the base and picked the bits of stone and dirt from our hair, our shoes, and even from out of our pockets. As we were busily dusting ourselves off, the search beam passed right in front of us. We sat quietly until the beam was over the hill, then we ran through the cornfield.

It started to rain, and we heard dogs barking in the distance. I was glad for the rain. It might prompt the soldiers and dogs to stay in the guardhouse a little longer. My wet shoes began to squelch in the muddy fields. I was afraid the noise would attract the dogs, so I took off my shoes and tried to walk barefoot through the corn stalks. But the sharp, freshly cut stalks pierced my already sore, tender feet. With each step, I couldn't help but let out a whimper of pain. We heard the dogs and the soldiers again, and we stood still in the middle of the field with the rain pouring down upon us. The search beam started panning the field, and we lay down in the mud. I forgot all about how much my feet hurt, and how cold and damp I was. We lay there without even breathing. I could feel Inchun's little body trembling in fear.

After a few minutes it was dark again, and there was only the sound of the pouring rain. I was thankful we had survived, and we kept walking. My feet were all bloody, and it was hard to keep silent. I moaned like a dying animal. After what seemed like several hours, we reached the foot of the hill. I looked at the ominous shadows the trees cast against the dense gray clouds. Inchun and I were drenched, and shivered in the darkness.

I was too scared and in too much pain to think or to say anything. Inchun pulled his little hand out of mine to wipe away his silent tears. I told him not to cry, and just to concentrate on putting one foot in front of the other. We started slipping in the mud as we tried to make our way up the hill. I clenched my teeth as I tried to get a foothold. It stopped raining, but the ground was still slippery. The dark branches loomed above and seemed as if they would reach out and grab us. We were all alone in the cold darkness. I couldn't feel the pain anymore. I felt numb.

We saw the searchlight over us again, but we were comforted that the trees were taller than we were. We stood still next to a big tree and we pretended to be a part of it. While we were waiting for the searchlight to pass the hill, we realized we had almost made it to the top. Far off in the distance, illuminated by the searchlight, was the barbed-wired fence.

I pulled Inchun's sleeve. "Look, do you see it? I think I can even see one or two little tents behind the fence, just as the old man said."

"I see it, too, *Nuna*," Inchun said.

We hurried up and over the hill, hoping we would be there soon. We slid down the hill most of the way, and were cut and bruised from falling on the rocks and twigs. The heavy clouds began to dissipate, and we kept running. We finally reached the bottom of the hill and looked ahead, hoping to see the barbed-wire fence in front of us as the old man had told us. But, instead, we heard the whispering of a swollen river, and up ahead I could see steel railroad tracks bridging the water.

We kept walking and finally reached the tracks, which would be our bridge to the South. The railroad ties of the tracks were made of wood and were spaced several feet apart. A grown-up would just be able to make it from one tie to the next. If we made one false move, we would fall into the rapidly flowing river, and would surely die. We looked in terror at the task ahead of us. Gripped with fear, we looked around. Now we could clearly see the barbed-wire fence and the well-lit tents ahead.

"*Nuna*, the old man said nothing about a river and rail-road tracks. We must be in the wrong place."

"Look," I said, "that is the South. We have to cross this river by going over these cross-rungs. Then we can run to the fence. The sky is lighter now and we can see better. Mother might be there waiting for us. I don't know if this is the right place, but I don't see another way."

Inchun stared at the railroad ties and cried. "Mommy, Mommy," he kept sobbing.

We sat there for a long time staring at the long distance between the railroad ties and the river below. "Well, Inchun, I think we can do it. Get down on all fours and stretch out your arms one at a time and try to grab onto the next rung. I'll go first and we'll take each step slowly and carefully. Don't look down. Make sure you grab the wooden bar with your hands first, then move your legs one at a time. You can hold on to my ankles. I'll grab onto the next rung and tell you when your hand and my ankle can move to the next one. Come on, there are the dogs and soldiers again." I had to reach out to grab the splintery rung, and my head started to spin when I looked at the dark turgid waters below. I was sure I would fall into the river, dragging Inchun with me.

Little Inchun looked at me and stretched his arms to reach the first rung. I turned and looked, and the gap between the rungs looked even larger than before; his little arms could barely reach. My whole body felt as if it were on fire. I was terribly afraid for him. He was brave. He said nothing, clenched his teeth with determination, and reached out to grab the rung and my ankle and carefully pull himself over. Rung by rung, we slowly continued. The light of dawn helped us to see the rungs. But the better we could see the path, the better the Russians would be able to see us. We kept crawling slowly from rung to rung until the land rose up beneath the tracks. We had crossed over the river and had about a quarter of a mile to go.

How inviting that barbed-wire fence seemed! Only that small distance separated us now. Mother might be waiting for us in one of those tents with the warm glowing lights. Inchun and I looked at each other and started running toward the fence. At any moment the Russian guards might spring upon us. It was misty and wet. We soon heard the fierce barking of dogs. They must have discovered our scent. We froze and stared at each other. The dogs were getting closer and closer and the barking grew louder and fiercer. We heard the soldiers' footsteps in the distance. We heard them shouting to one another.

It wasn't worth trying to hide anymore. It was now or never. We could see the fence right in front of us. We locked our hands together and ran as fast as we could. We just ran and ran, and finally reached the barbed-wire fence. Using all my remaining strength, I pulled at the bottom of the wire. It would not budge. There was no time to think. We fell to our knees and started to dig. We only made a tiny little space. Then I tried to lift the fence as much as I could. "Go, Inchun!" I urged. "Flatten yourself out like a snake and slide through, then keep running. I'll be right behind you."

Little Inchun slipped under the wire and then, instead of running as I had told him, he tried to lift the wire with his little hands. I heard the dogs drawing closer and I thrust my body under the wire. The barbs dug into me. My hair was caught, my clothes ripped, and I could feel the blood pooling in the cuts on my back. I kept going, and finally, I made it through. I grabbed Inchun's hand. We cried and kept running.

I did not look back to see how close the soldiers and the dogs were. I was too afraid. I could only look forward.

Inchun said, panting, "Are we in the South now?"

"Yes," I said, clutching his hand tighter.

"But I still hear the dogs and the soldiers," Inchun said.

"Don't worry, just run!" I squeezed his hand and pulled him forward. I had heard that once you were in the South, the Russians and the North Koreans could not shoot you, even if you were an escapee. But still we ran. They sounded as though they were right behind us. We kept running toward the lit tents. Then I saw four people rushing out of the tents and running to us. I saw the Red Cross sign on their white hats. They were carrying stretchers and medical bags, and I finally felt that we didn't have to run anymore.

I stopped and grabbed Inchun. "We can stop now," I told him. "We're safe, we're safe." My trembling legs collapsed under me and I fell to the ground. Inchun tumbled down on top of me. Exhaustion and relief overwhelmed us. I looked at him, and his eyes were closed. I felt dizzy and looked up at the sky, which was spinning above me. As I was lifted onto a stretcher, my eyes filled with tears. I heard the soothing voice of an older woman saying, "These poor children . . . all alone . . . Look at their feet. Hurry, let's get them inside. Hurry."

Epilogue

Inchun and I must have slept for days at the Red Cross center at the 38th Parallel. By the time we awoke, the information center had located our father's address in Seoul. The nurse fed us and bandaged our feet, and said she would put us on the bus to Seoul when we were ready. Anxious to see whether Mother was already at home waiting for us, we decided to leave on the very next bus. Clutching the little piece of paper with our new address, we rode down the dusty, bumpy country roads.

We made our way through the noisy, bustling streets of Seoul, and asked with nervous excitement for directions to our house at 23 Ulgiro 4-ka. We finally found the house and stepped through the open front door. Father and our three older brothers, sitting at the dinner table, were shocked to see us and immediately asked where Mother was.

She was not there waiting for us as we had hoped, and Father had received no news of her. Sad, exhausted, and still suffering from fever and infected cuts, Inchun and I remained in bed for several weeks recuperating.

When we recovered, Father enrolled us at the Younghi School near our house. It was strangely comforting to meet many other girls like me who had come from the North and were still waiting for members of their families. A group of us started a poetry club, and befriended and comforted each other as we waited day after day.

Meanwhile, Father started a soy sauce factory in the city of Inchon. He offered shelter and employment to many refugees from the North, and the factory became an information center and meeting place of sorts for refugees. Father tried to get every bit of news he could that might help us find out about Mother.

Our oldest brother, Hanchun, was attending the veterinary school at Seoul University and would bring sick dogs, birds, and even monkeys home on weekends to nurse back to health. Jaechun was still recovering from tuberculosis, which he had contracted in the Japanese labor camps; he only went to the university in the mornings, and in the afternoons, he stayed home, listening to classical music and reading. Hyunchun had decided he wanted to be a diplomat and was studying at the Foreign Language University.

Inchun and I liked our new school, and liked being home with all our brothers. But each day, we prayed that Mother would join us. After six long months, Mother suddenly appeared at the house. She was supposed to have been shipped to a labor camp in Siberia with the others who had been caught trying to escape. But one of the Russian colonels who lived near the border town needed someone to cook and clean for his young wife, who was expecting their first child. Mother became their housekeeper and governess. They forbade her to speak to anyone or to go beyond the front gate of the house, and soldiers often patrolled the area. But one foggy, drizzly afternoon, she decided to walk out and try to make it to the border. She had no specific plan, and she didn't know where she would be able to get across. She couldn't stand it there another minute without us, she said, and decided to risk everything. It was a miracle, she told us. No one saw her in the dense monsoon fog, and she walked and walked. She stumbled in a pile of branches and leaves, and fell deep into a small tunnel. She saw a glimmer of light at the other end and crawled toward it, without knowing where it was leading. When she reached the end, she found she had tunneled under the barbed-wire fence and was on the southern side of the 38th Parallel. We later found out it was one of many secret tunnels the Communists were constructing to invade the South.

With Mother safe and at home in Seoul, life in the South was almost everything I had ever hoped for. But each day we still longed to hear some word of Kisa, Aunt Tiger, my sister, Theresa, and the sock girls.

Our freedom and happiness did not last long. In June 1950, war broke out. North Korean and Communist soldiers filled the streets of Seoul, and were soon joined by Chinese Communist troops. Russian tanks came barreling through. In the chaos, many more North Korean refugees made their way to Seoul. Theresa and the other nuns finally escaped, and made their way to our house. They told us that the Russians and Town Reds had found out about Kisa's and Aunt Tiger's other activities. They died as all "traitors" did. They were shot with machine guns, and then hanged in the town square to serve as a lesson to others. We never heard any further news about the sock girls, or about my friend Unhi. I still wonder if they are alive in the North.

About the Author

Born in Pyongyang, North Korea, Sook Nyul Choi immigrated to the United States to pursue her college education. After graduating from Manhattanville College, she taught in New York City schools for almost twenty years while raising her two daughters. She now resides in Cambridge, Massachusetts, where she devotes most of her time to her writing.